Allen & Mike's
AVALANCHE
BOOK

Skills & techniques with cartoons!

Allen & Mike's
AVALANCHE
BOOK

A guide to staying safe in avalanche terrain

Allen O'Bannon
With illustrations by **Mike Clelland!**

FALCONGUIDES

GUILFORD, CONNECTICUT
HELENA, MONTANA

AN IMPRINT OF GLOBE PEQUOT PRESS

To buy books in quantity for corporate use or incentives, call **(800) 962-0973** or e-mail **premiums@GlobePequot.com**.

FALCONGUIDES®

FalconGuides is an imprint of Globe Pequot Press.

Falcon, FalconGuides, and Outfit Your Mind are registered trademarks of Morris Book Publishing, LLC.

All illustrations by Mike Clelland unless otherwise noted.

Library of Congress Cataloging-in-Publication Data is available on file.

ISBN 978-0-7627-7999-4

Printed in the United States of America

Contents

Acknowledgments

Wow, where would I start? There are so many people to thank. Let's start with all my ski partners, thanks for putting up with me, give me a call when it starts snowing; all the instructors I have taught courses with, thanks for sharing so much of your knowledge and those Powerpoint slides. To Ian McCammon for all the research, thoughts, and good conversations; Dale Atkins for the ideas on how to think beyond ourselves; Don Sharaf for being Don Sharaf; Mike Clelland, of course, for drawings, ideas, and so much more; and Molly Absolon for all the help you gave me on this project and everything else—I love you.

Introduction

Avalanches are a hard thing to predict. First off, you have to know what one is. After that there is a steep learning curve to assimilate all the information involved in predicting whether a slope is stable or not. Even then, avalanche professionals will tell you that while there are times they know things are going to slide and there are times when they are sure things are stable, there still exists a big gray area where you can never be 100 percent confident you know what is going to happen. This is why even the experts get caught in avalanches from time to time, and why no one really wants to be considered an expert even if they are.

Our goal in putting together this book is to help you enjoy being out in the snow—skiing, snowboarding, or however you like to recreate (maybe by snowmobile, snowshoe, or some other form unknown to us, although we won't really make references to these because we don't have much experience with them). Mike and I certainly can't make you an expert or even ensure your safety, but hopefully we can add some information to your knowledge bank to help you make better decisions.

When it comes to increasing your avalanche knowledge, books can only take you so far. Nothing is going to beat experience. Your best bet is to take an avalanche course, or even two avalanche courses. Find a mentor who can share his or her experiences with you (keeping in mind that even the experts make mistakes) and just get out there in the snow. There are strategies to being safe even on the most horrendous of days; in fact, sometimes the best learning comes when an avalanche is actually happening because you get direct experience—just avoid *being* that experience.

We tried to organize this book in the way we go about approaching a day of skiing to help you develop the habits of thinking about snow, weather, terrain, and your own fallibility. Good habits are important to learning any skill, and they can help keep you safe because you follow them unconsciously. Routine is really one of our best lines of defense. Of course, we couldn't find a way to include everything you might encounter in a day of skiing, but we tried to hit the most common scenarios.

Keep in mind that the field of avalanche forecasting is continually evolving. We are trying to share with you what is most relevant today, but the fact is, in a few years better tests may have come along, the way people characterize how a fracture starts may change, and what is considered important to know about snow structure could be different. With that in mind we will try to stick to general principles and avoid going too in depth on any subject. If you are a real stickler for details and want to gain a deeper knowledge of all the science behind this, then your best bet is to take more advanced avalanche courses, read the papers and others books being written by avalanche professionals and researchers, and search out the myriad opportunities available for learning more about snow (see our list of resources in the appendix).

First a Story

A few years ago my ski partner was caught in an avalanche. I was behind the rollover and couldn't see the slope below, but I heard him yell. I remember my stomach lurching and my palms sweating as I side-slipped to the edge to look down. The avalanche was small, but the snow had piled up in a gully below, and I saw no sign of my partner. I told myself to be calm, to do what I knew how to do, and pulled out my transceiver. Before I even switched the unit to search mode, my friend's hand punched out through the debris pile and waved back and forth. I felt an immense sense of relief as I shoved my transceiver back into my pocket and skidded down the slope. He was alive, and I knew where he was. Within a minute or two, I had uncovered his head.

We were lucky, but humbled. Both of us were outdoor professionals, trained in avalanche forecasting and accustomed to leading groups into the backcountry in the winter. But on that day we'd fallen into a number of classic traps: We'd failed to take note of the rising temperatures and ignored the fact that we'd switched aspects, seen shooting cracks, and skied into a terrain trap. But perhaps most notably, we'd been seduced by the swath of untracked powder on a day when most of the surrounding slopes had been blasted by the wind and sun.

Every year people are caught and, in some cases, killed in avalanches. Why? Usually it's a combination of factors: ignorance of the risk, pushing the limits of what's safe to ski, a belief they can manage or outsmart the snowpack, or like us, blinded in their decision-making by their desire.

While we hope to help you develop a system for making decisions in avalanche terrain, we also want you to recognize that the desire to ski some great snow or an awesome line often trumps our ability to make rational decisions. Figuring out a way to see around this desire is one of the greatest challenges of avalanche education and safety.

SOME OF THE BASICS

Okay, we need to touch on a number of basics before we can head out and go skiing in avalanche terrain or we really won't even know what to look for. First off, we use the metric system for most of the measurements included in this book because it's the industry standard in the avalanche-forecasting field. If you have forgotten how big a centimeter is, just remember that 10 centimeters equates to roughly 4 inches. That's not exact, but close enough.

30cm = 0.98425 FEET

What Is an Avalanche?

An avalanche is a sudden flow of snow down a slope that occurs when a trigger—either a natural trigger like new snow

---

Exceptions

One very important thing to keep in mind as you read this book—and when you are out skiing—is to look for the exceptions. Just because we give you some rule of thumb, like the angles that slab avalanches typically run on, doesn't mean there won't be exceptions to the rule. Avalanches have been known to run on lower angles; in fact, people in different regions may give you different parameters for these angles.

There are a lot of variables associated with avalanches, so exceptions should be expected. Also, as you gain experience skiing in an area, you will get comfortable with certain conditions. It is often in a year when conditions are very different that people start getting caught in avalanches. Be on the lookout for exceptions to what you are used to.

Even a small **SLUFF** can sweep you into more **DANGEROUS TERRAIN**

Yikes!

SWOOOSH!

or an artificial trigger like a skier—overloads the snowpack. Avalanches come in all shapes and sizes and have a correspondingly wide range of destructive capacity. They can bury towns, take out roads, and kill scores of people, or they can simply move a small pocket of unstable snow a few inches.

For our purposes avalanches can be divided into two categories: loose-snow slides, or sluffs, and slab avalanches.

Sluffs

Sluffs only involve the top layer of loose, powdery snow. They start from a single point—hence the reason they are also known as point release avalanches—and entrain more and more snow as they move downhill. In the process a single sluff creates a characteristic teardrop shape. Often skiers on a slope will trigger numerous sluffs as

they descend, and as a result the teardrop shape is not always evident.

Skiers and boarders commonly trigger sluffs on slopes steeper than 40 degrees. As more and more athletes venture into such terrain, it is becoming standard practice to consciously manage or mitigate sluffs to avoid injury. The real danger is not getting buried, as sluffs do not typically result in big pileups of snow. Rather the hazard is being knocked over by the snow and injured in a high-speed fall or being pushed over cliffs and into obstacles.

Sluff management is accomplished in several ways. One is to ski back and forth across the slope, working your way downhill in a series of traversing lines. This technique, however, doesn't allow for much fun skiing and mars the aesthetic purity of untracked powder. If you want to get some turns in, you can manage your sluff through speed—skiing faster or slower than the moving snow. The terrain and your ability will dictate whether it is better to go fast or slow. A conservative approach is to make a few turns, stop and let the snow pass you, then continue downhill.

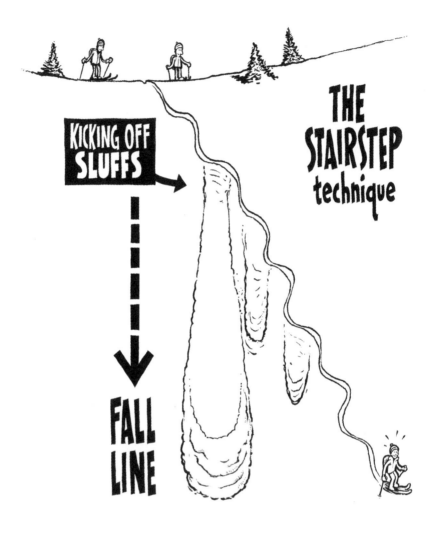

KICKING OFF SLUFFS

FALL LINE

THE STAIRSTEP technique

You can also manage your sluff by moving laterally across the slope and out of the slide path with each turn as you descend. This stairstep technique demands a certain amount of space to be effective.

Slab Avalanches

For most backcountry travelers, slab avalanches are the biggest avalanche hazard and account for almost all avalanche fatalities. They are the big killers and the ones we will focus on in this book.

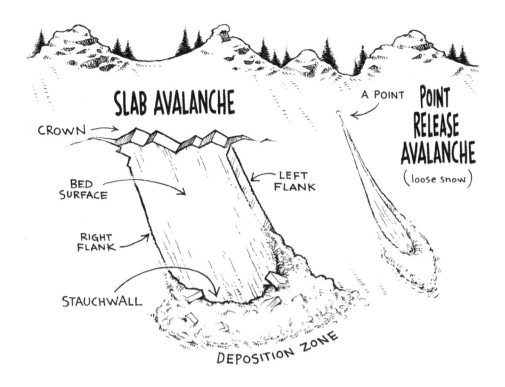

SLAB AVALANCHE

CROWN

BED
SURFACE

LEFT
FLANK

RIGHT
FLANK

STAUCHWALL

DEPOSITION ZONE

A POINT

POINT
RELEASE
AVALANCHE
(loose snow)

A slab is a layer of snow held together by internal bonds that are stronger than the bonds attaching it to the snow below.

Slabs become a problem when they sit on a weak layer over a sliding surface on a slope with enough angle to allow the snow to move. That angle starts around 25 degrees and increases until it gets so steep the snow just slides off. However, most avalanches occur between 30 and 50 degrees, with the prime angle falling between 35 to 40 degrees (38 degrees is commonly considered the magic number for most avalanches).

CLOSE UP
X-RAY
VIEW

IMAGINE
THE FRAGILE
LAYER AS
CHAMPAGNE
GLASSES

WEAK
LAYER
FAILS

CRACK!

RAPID
LOADING

NEW SNOW

DENSE SLABBY
LAYER

MOVING

DENSE SNOW
as bed surface

Loading can be from new snow adding stress to the snowpack. A skier or snow machine adds stress as well.

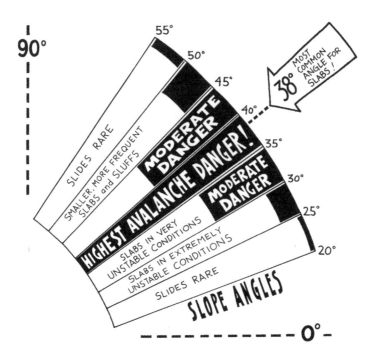

X-RAY CROSS SECTION

Slab avalanches can be further categorized as dry and wet, and soft and hard. Wet slides can run on lower-angle slopes (down to 20 degrees or less in extreme cases, such as with a slush avalanche) and are most common in the spring when you have free water in the snowpack. If it's not freezing at night, beware! That's when wet slides typically occur.

Isothermal Snowpack

An isothermal snowpack is one in which the snowpack measures 0 degrees Celsius (freezing) from top to bottom, a phenomenon that typically occurs in the spring when you have warm days with intense solar radiation and nights where the temperature fails to fall below freezing. Under these conditions snow begins to melt and water runs down through the pack, dissolving the bonds between grains that give the snowpack its strength. The result is a rotten snowpack with no internal cohesion—a pack that fails easily, resulting in wet avalanches. You'll recognize an isothermal snowpack; it's the one that gives you no support, where you punch through to the ground even on skis. When you experience these kinds of conditions, it's time to get off the slope.

PLOPPY BOMBS

INTENSE WARMING during the day

} ISOTHERMAL SLOP!

Remember that wet slides can run on lower-angle slopes than dry slab avalanches. Pay attention to above-freezing overnight temperatures if you plan to head out in the spring, and watch out when you start punching through. These are all danger signs.

Dry slabs are more common in the middle of winter when layers form in the snowpack as a result of storm cycles, droughts, cold snaps, heat waves, wind, and sun. Some of these factors strengthen the snowpack while others weaken it; all of them create patterns that affect a slope's stability.

If you could watch a slab detach in slow motion, you'd see that it moves initially as one unified plate of snow. This layer quickly breaks up into blocks (big, hard blocks in hard slabs; softer, smaller pieces in soft ones). The crown, flanks, and stauchwall are all part of the avalanche's starting zone. It then flows down the slide track, ending up in the deposition zone or toe of the avalanche.

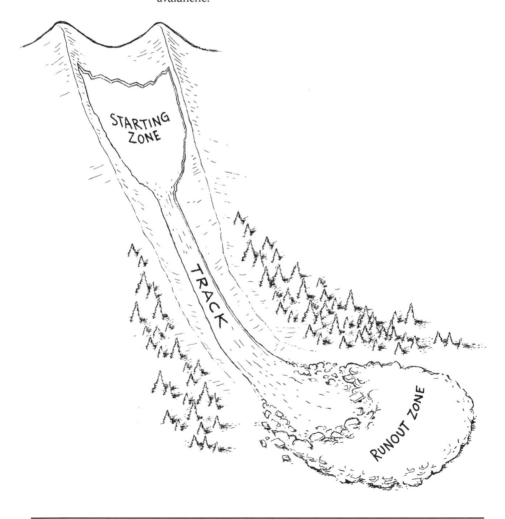

The Avalanche Triangle

In 1984 Doug Fesler and Jill Fredston published the first edition of *Snow Sense*, a book that quickly became a kind of Bible for beginning avalanche students. The beauty of *Snow Sense* was its practicality. Fesler and Fredston created a model—the avalanche triangle—for interpreting data that is simple to use and easy to remember. Their triangle continues to be used by avalanche educators around the world today.

The avalanche triangle divides objective information into three categories: terrain, weather, and snowpack. Each category is considered individually, and a color—red, yellow, or green—is assigned to it. So, for example, if you were evaluating the hazard of the terrain at your local golf course, you would give it a green light. The terrain is not capable of producing a slide; therefore it is not a problem, and you have a green light to go skiing out there.

Of course, in real backcountry terrain the question is almost never that simple, but you get the general idea of how the process works. Green means go, red means stop, and yellow means caution—things are not really clear. To further complicate the situation, you may experience a variety of yellowish conditions. For example, the terrain can be yellowish green and the weather yellowish red. Avalanche assessment is rarely cut and dried. You often find yourself forced to make decisions based on conflicting or unclear information.

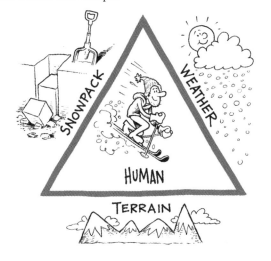

In the center of the avalanche triangle, Fesler and Fredston put the human factor, or the more nebulous subjective factors that influence decision-making in the backcountry. The idea is to ask a series of questions about your specific group and goals to help determine where you should or shouldn't ski—in the same way you ask questions about terrain, weather, and snowpack.

Terrain

When we first started backcountry skiing in leather boots on skinny telemark skis, it was easy to be perfectly content on low-angle slopes. But as the gear improved and stiff plastic boots and fat skis came along, 20- to 30-degree slopes were no longer challenging enough. People nowadays commonly ski

35-plus-degree slopes, which of course is where most avalanches occur.

Slope Angle

Slope angle is the single most important factor in considering whether or not the terrain is capable of producing a slide. Unfortunately, most of us aren't that good at guessing slope angle. The best way to determine slope angle is to measure it. Carry an inclinometer (a slope meter) with you when you go touring and measure the angle of your favorite slopes. And remember, if you are an advanced or expert skier and the slope looks fun to ski, chances are it's steep enough to slide.

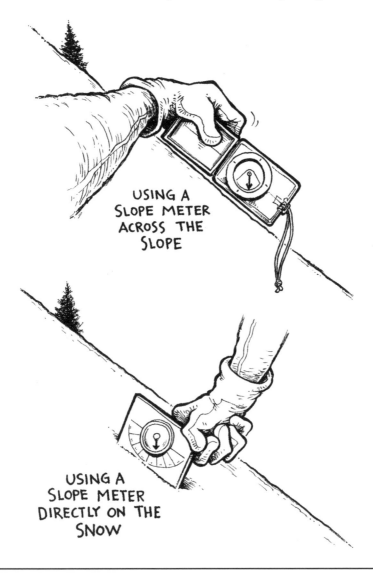

USING A SLOPE METER ACROSS THE SLOPE

USING A SLOPE METER DIRECTLY ON THE SNOW

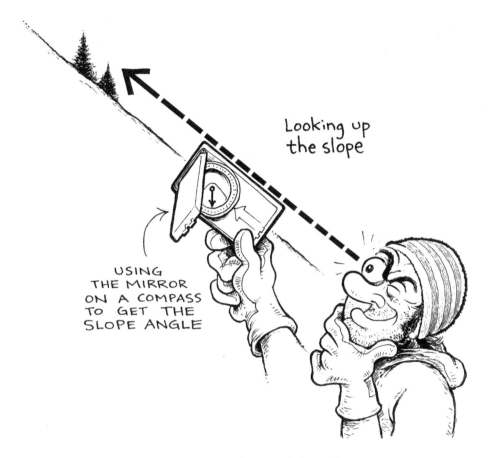

Looking up
the slope

USING
THE MIRROR
ON A COMPASS
TO GET THE
SLOPE ANGLE

Beware: No one is perfect at measuring slopes, and the angles you measure will probably be off a few degrees one way or another. If you are trying to stay off anything over 30 degrees on a day when the avalanche danger is through the roof, be sure to compensate for this.

Slope Aspect

A slope's aspect determines its sun exposure and the effect wind has on it. Overall, north-facing slopes tend to be more prone to avalanches because the snow is colder and slower to bond together. You are also more likely to get "faceting" on north-facing slopes. We'll go into detail on facets later, but for now you just need to know that facets result in sugary, weak snow that can be a perfect weak/sliding layer for a slab.

While slopes with northerly aspects (at least those north of the equator; this is reversed for the southern hemisphere) remain cold, slopes with south-facing aspects often develop a sun crust that can act as the sliding layer.

Moderate warming on a slope will strengthen and stabilize the snowpack, but sudden dramatic rises in temperature from the sun can have the opposite effect. Many avalanches occur when slopes are exposed to intense solar radiation, especially in the spring or after a big storm.

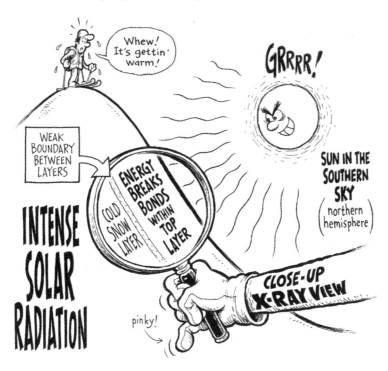

Wind is a critical and often underestimated factor in a slope's avalanche potential. When you've just received a 6-inch dump, it's easy to think, yippee, fresh turns. But if that dump was accompanied by 30 mph winds, you are looking at much more than 6 new inches of fresh snow on the lee slopes. There may be 2 feet or more in wind-loaded areas, which is more than enough to create a worrisome slab. Winds can move snow ten times faster than simple precipitation. So pay attention to which aspects are loading and be wary.

Wind-affected snow exhibits some obvious signs. On scoured, windward slopes you'll find evidence of sastrugi or sculpted snow that is firm and looks like terrible skiing. On wind-loaded leeward slopes, the signs are subtler: The snow often looks chalky or dull because the wind has broken up the crystals that glint in the sun. You'll see evidence of pillows—smooth, rounded layers of snow. If you venture out onto wind slab, the snow will feel stiff and will often crack. In some cases it can even feel hard and hollow. All these are signs of wind loading, which means bad or dangerous skiing.

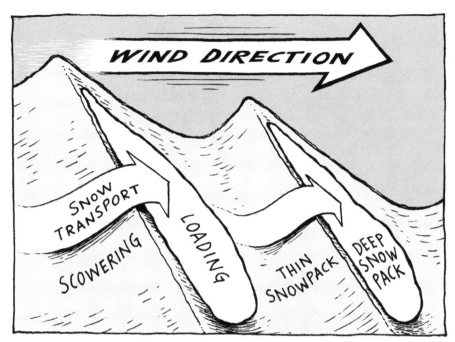

CROSS LOADING

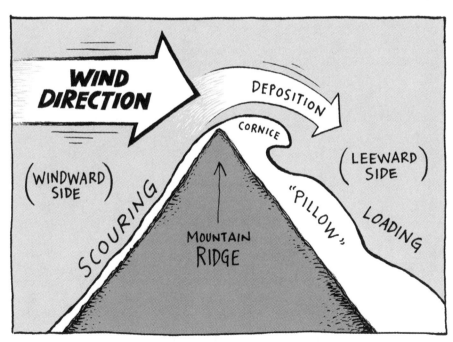

WIND LOADING

Slope Shape

A slope's shape also affects its ability to slide. Avalanches often fracture at convexities—the rollover where the stress on the snow is greatest. Concave slopes have some compressive support at the base that can help stabilize the snow, but be careful. This compressive support is usually only a mitigating factor on small slopes. Big concavities like the infamous Glory Bowl on Teton Pass are prime avalanche paths. They are too big for any stabilization to result from the compression at the base of the bowl.

Slope Texture/Anchors

Finally, the roughness of a slope affects its sliding ability. Think of a metal roof versus one made from asphalt shingles. Snow slides off metal roofs easier than it does off shingles even if the load is the same. In the mountains this roughness can come from underlying vegetation, boulders, or uneven snow surfaces. Trees can act as anchors helping to hold the snow in place. But again, use caution. Anchors are only effective if there are enough of them. You'll commonly hear the saying; "Trees are only safe if they are too close together to ski." Even this saying has its limitations. If a slope above the trees slides, suddenly the trees you thought were your protection become hazardous as you are carried down between them.

Rock outcroppings can also be a mixed bag, anchoring the snow in some conditions and becoming sweet spots (areas from which avalanches are often triggered) in others. Isolated trees and rocks can actually weaken the snowpack because they create areas of tension (as the snow around them slowly creeps downhill) and cause faceting, forming weak pockets, or gardens, of snow that can become the starting zone for a slide.

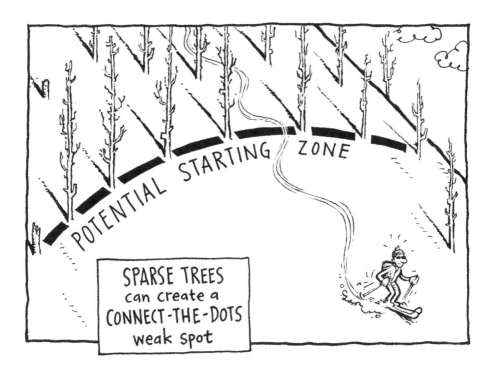

POTENTIAL STARTING ZONE

SPARSE TREES can create a CONNECT-THE-DOTS weak spot

Reading Terrain Clues

Vegetation and terrain can tell you the story of a slope's past if you look closely. Swaths of open areas funneling into gullies are classic avalanche slopes that are easy to recognize. But there are more subtle signs you can observe as well. Look for "disaster species"—alders or willows—small flexible plants that can withstand the impact of sliding snow. Note any marked difference in the size of the slope's trees, which indicates it has slid enough times in the past to prevent large, climax species from getting established. Notice if trees are bent or broken, or only have branches on the downhill side. These are all warning signs that the slope has slid in the past and can slide again in the future.

Learning to recognize avalanche terrain is a critical route-finding skill. You can travel in the backcountry when the avalanche hazard is high if you know how to choose a safe route. In unfamiliar terrain it helps to line out a route on a topographic map at home. This allows you to identify potential trouble spots and safety zones. Look out for gullies—or terrain traps where snow can pile up deeply—and watch to make sure your route doesn't take you below big, steep avalanche slopes.

Avalanche Terrain Exposure Scale

Developed by Canadian avalanche forecasters, the avalanche terrain exposure scale (ATES) is a useful tool for assessing the hazard level of any given terrain.

- *Simple terrain* has exposure to low-angle, mostly forested, rolling or flat terrain. You may encounter the runout zones of an infrequent avalanche path in simple terrain, but there are plenty of ways to reduce or avoid exposure.

- *Challenging terrain* has exposure to well-defined avalanche paths, starting zones, and terrain traps. You can reduce or avoid exposure to these hazards with careful route-finding, but you need skill and experience to recognize the danger.

- *Complex terrain* has exposure to multiple, overlapping avalanche paths or large expanses of steep, open terrain with multiple avalanche starting zones and numerous terrain traps. Complex terrain has very few or no options to avoid or reduce exposure.

Use the avalanche terrain exposure scale in conjunction with your morning assessment of current avalanche and weather conditions to decide where to ski. On days when you feel confident in the snow's stability, plan a tour in challenging or complex terrain. On days when there is a lot of concern about the avalanche hazard, stick to simple terrain.

SIMPLE

CHALLENGING

COMPLEX

AVALANCHE TERRAIN

Weather

Weather constantly changes the snowpack. For those of us who want to travel in avalanche terrain, the question is, how is the weather affecting the snow's strength?

Past Weather

Weather can be broken down into past, current, and future. Past weather describes what you are likely to find buried beneath the surface of the snow. It includes everything that has happened since the first storm in the fall left snow on the ground. Past weather leaves behind clues you can see when you dig a pit down into the snowpack. It's that November rain crust, the depth hoar from December's long drought, or the January surface hoar layer. The layers will have different densities or

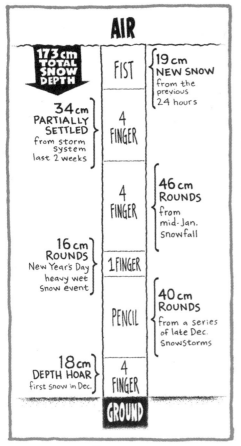

mostly GOOD layering

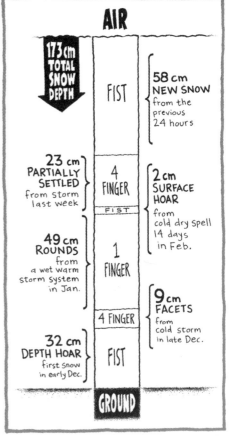

some BAD layers

hardness as well—some will be easy to stick a fist into while others may be so hard they may be classified as pencil hard. More on this in chapter 4. Avalanche geeks will often be able to recall specific dates for each distinct layer.

If you go to a new area where you aren't familiar with the weather's history, ask the locals what's been going on. Most years have had a few significant events that are worth being aware of before you head out to ski. If you can't get that information, dig a bunch of pits. After a while you'll recognize certain layers—say an old rain crust or a layer of surface hoar—that could affect the snow's stability.

Current Weather

The question for current weather is, how is it affecting the snowpack now? Most natural avalanches occur during or immediately after a storm, but what is it about a storm that makes this happen?

First, consider precipitation. How much snow is falling? Is it heavy or light? Is it coming down fast? How long has it been snowing? How much has accumulated? Is the temperature rising or falling?

Heavy snowfall—more than 1 inch per hour for 6 hours or more, or more than 12 inches in 24 hours—increases the load on the snowpack, adding stress. Warm, wet snow is heavier than cold, dry powder because of its increased water content, which means it adds even more load.

RED LIGHT WEATHER

The wind is also a factor in precipitation because it moves snow, loading slopes, sometimes when there is no snow falling from the sky. Winds under 20 mph are typically not strong enough to transport snow that is already on the ground, but once they get over 20 mph, watch out. If it's blowing, you don't need a lot of new snow to load a slope.

Finally, temperature affects avalanche conditions. The temperatures we are talking about include the ambient temperature, the snowpack temperature, and any solar radiation that might be taking place.

Warming temperatures are a double-edged sword. Rapid warming temporarily destabilizes the snowpack. Why? Because it messes up the snowpack's internal balance. Snow is always

Some of the Basics

moving downhill in response to the pull of gravity. Called creep, this process is normal and usually not a problem. But when you have rapid heating, the top layers of snow settle more quickly than normal and begin creeping downhill faster than the snow below, thereby adding stress to the snowpack.

RAPIDLY WARMING SNOW CREEP

Slow warming, on the other hand, encourages bonding in the snowpack and, over time, makes it more stable.

Long periods of cold, clear weather can result in weak snow on the surface (surface hoar or near-surface faceting) and, with shallow or early season snowpacks, can lead to the formation of depth hoar—another weak, potentially dangerous layer—near the ground.

Future Weather

I generally check the avalanche forecast and weather before I head out for a ski day to get a sense of what happened overnight and what's predicted for the day. Red flags include new snow, high winds either overnight or in the forecast, and rapid warming during the day. Once I get out in the field, I'll start looking around to see how applicable the forecast is to my location. Remember that mountains create their own microclimates. Avalanche forecasts are general and written to cover a broad area. I know that what is happening at my house at 8 a.m. may not be what is happening at the top of a mountain a few miles away at that same hour. So use the information you glean from the forecast to inform—not make—your decisions.

Snowpack

The final side of the avalanche triangle is the snowpack. To create a slab avalanche, the snowpack must have a slab, a weak layer, and a bed surface. What makes snow strong or weak, slippery or bonded, is often determined by how it changes once it hits the ground. These changes, known as metamorphism, either create strong internal cohesion in the snowpack in a process known as rounding, or destroy bonds in a process known as faceting, resulting in loose, sugary snow.

SNOW FALLS
from the sky

BURIED SNOW
begins rounding

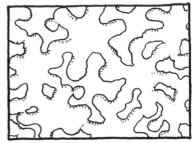

ROUNDING PROCESS
begins within
crystals

rounding and
settlement create
STRONG BONDS

Some of the Basics

Avalanche Climate Characteristics

Maritime: Mountains Bordering Oceans

- Deep snowpack (more than 3 meters)
- Warm temperatures (-5 to 5 degrees Celsius) (23 to 41 degrees Fahrenheit)
- High-density snow (10 to 20 percent water by volume)
- Frequent storms with lots of snow
- Weak layers are less pronounced and usually do not persist
- Avalanches generally occurring during storms, triggered by precipitation or wind
- Midwinter rain common
- Wet slides possible throughout the year

Intermountain: Mountains with Limited Ocean Influence

- Intermediate snowpack depths (1.5 to 3 meters)
- Intermediate temperatures (-15 to -3 degrees Celsius) (5 to 27 degrees Fahrenheit)
- Weak layers are present and can include variations in new snow as well as persistent weak layers such as surface hoar or facets
- Instabilities can remain for several days after a storm and may linger for long periods, especially when coupled with persistent weak layers and cold temperatures.
- Midwinter rain can happen, but rarely

Continental: Mountains Far from the Influence of Oceans

- Thin snowpack (less than 1.5 meters)
- Cold temperatures (-30 to -10 degrees Celsius) (-22 to 14 degrees Fahrenheit)
- Storms characterized by small accumulations of low-density snow
- Persistent weak layers like surface hoar and depth hoar are common and can linger for an entire season in extreme situations.
- Midwinter rain extremely rare

Note: The boundaries between avalanche climates are fluid and can change during the course of a season or from year to year. You may even find variations within a single mountain range, where one side has a deep snowpack that looks maritime, while the other side is dry and the snowpack thin like that found in a continental snowpack.

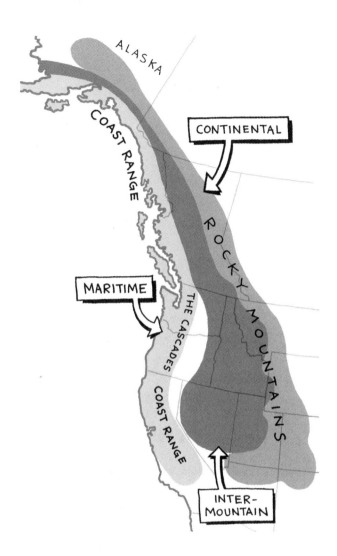

Rounding

Rounding occurs in deep snow with relatively warm temperatures. The key is that there is no temperature gradient—or dramatic variation in temperatures—within the snowpack. In the absence of a temperature gradient, snow crystals gradually lose their points and edges, slowly deteriorating into small, rounded grains that are bonded together. Rounding strengthens the snowpack, but as always there is a potential downside to the phenomena: Rounding also creates slabs. If a well-bonded slab of rounded snow is lying on top of a weak layer, it can be dangerous. But in general, rounding is good for overall stability.

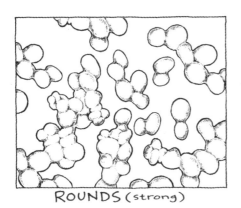

ROUNDS (strong)

FACETS (weak)

Faceting

Faceting occurs when there is a temperature gradient in the snowpack. As a general rule this gradient averages a change of 1 degree Celsius or more per 10 centimeters, although it can vary depending on the ambient temperature and the depth of the snowpack.

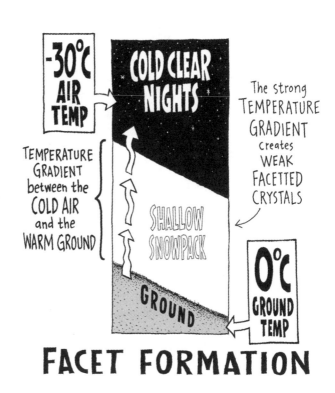

-30°C AIR TEMP

COLD CLEAR NIGHTS

The strong TEMPERATURE GRADIENT creates WEAK FACETTED CRYSTALS

TEMPERATURE GRADIENT between the COLD AIR and the WARM GROUND

SHALLOW SNOWPACK

GROUND

0°C GROUND TEMP

FACET FORMATION

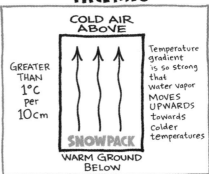

ROUNDING

COLD AIR ABOVE

LESS THAN 1°C per 10cm

SNOWPACK

WARM GROUND BELOW

weak temperature gradient so water vapor can move in ALL DIRECTIONS

FACETING

COLD AIR ABOVE

GREATER THAN 1°C per 10cm

SNOWPACK

WARM GROUND BELOW

Temperature gradient is so strong that water vapor MOVES UPWARDS towards colder temperatures

SNOW CRYSTALS CHANGE
within the snowpack
DUE TO TEMPERATURE GRADIENT

For the nerdy folks among us it should be noted that it is really a vapor pressure gradient that determines faceting and rounding. However it is much easier to measure the temperature gradient than vapor pressure and since the two are related it works well.

Deep snowpacks lessen the chance of a temperature gradient developing by creating more distance between the warm ground—which averages 0 degrees Celsius or the freezing temperature—and the cold air. The classic faceting scenario occurs when you have a shallow snowpack and cold temperatures. Faceting results in the formation of angular grains of snow that have very little internal cohesion. You can pick up a handful of faceted snow and it will flow out of your hand like sand.

Faceting can occur at any level in the snowpack. Depth hoar, which is the name for facets found at the ground-snow interface, is usually where you'll find the biggest, most angular grains. It's pretty easy to recognize depth hoar. You may have tried breaking trail in the stuff at some point. It's almost impossible to make much progress in depth hoar because the snow crumbles and collapses under your weight. It can do the same under a slab.

The bigger the facets are, the more difficult it is for them to switch their metamorphic process and begin to round should conditions change in the snowpack. This is why depth hoar formed in November can be a persistent problem throughout the rest of the winter.

Faceting can also occur at the surface. Called near-surface faceting, these grains of snow can be just as dangerous as depth hoar and are often a bit more difficult to detect since they usually don't grow as large. Near-surface faceting is the process that "refreshes" the powder on cold nights when there has been no new snow. Near-surface facets can make for great skiing but tend to sluff more than fresh powder snow. In fact, you know near-surface facets are forming when it hasn't snowed in a long while, yet the skiing on north-facing slopes is staying good or even getting better. Once a layer of near-surface facets gets buried, it will act as a weak layer. Well-developed layers of near-surface facets can also become a persistent or long-term weak layer in the snowpack.

Surface Hoar

Another important weak layer in the snowpack is surface hoar. Surface hoar is formed by water vapor condensing on the

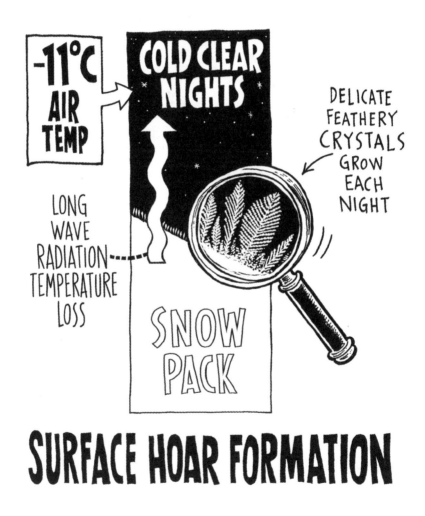

SURFACE HOAR FORMATION

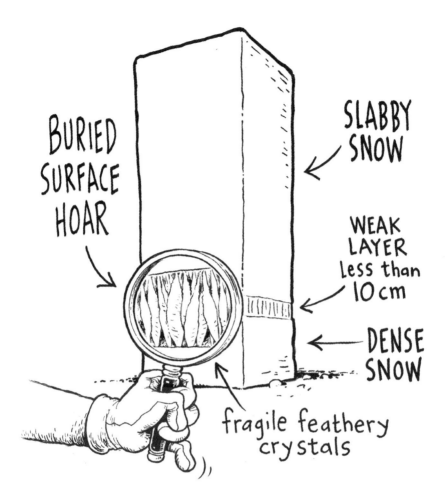

BURIED SURFACE HOAR

SLABBY SNOW

WEAK LAYER Less than 10 cm

DENSE SNOW

fragile feathery crystals

surface of the snow, like dew in the summer. The process creates feathery, flat crystals that sparkle in the sun and make a lovely, tinkly sound when you ski through them.

The ideal conditions for surface hoar formation are cold, clear, still nights with a very slight breeze. Surface hoar looks fragile, but in reality it is one of the most dangerous weak layers in a snowpack because it can persist for months and is often difficult to detect. The crystals stand on edge until something—maybe you jumping onto the slope—causes one grain to topple, and suddenly the whole layer collapses like a house of cards. Surface hoar is responsible for a large percentage of avalanche fatalities. I always make note of it when I see it forming and then look for it after it gets buried. When conditions are right, surface hoar can become quite large and will form a very obvious layer in the snowpack.

Whumping

When weak layers like surface hoar, depth hoar, or near-surface faceting collapse, you'll know it. The whole snowpack seems to drop and you hear a "whumping" noise. That's nature screaming at you: "Danger, danger, Will Robinson!" (Okay, I've probably just made a reference that predates most of you, but you get my drift.)

Why is whumping dangerous? Because it is the sound of a weak layer failing under the stress of a load—namely you. Under the right conditions that failure could cause an avalanche. It definitely means there is a weak layer under the surface that is reactive to added weight.

WHUMP!

(an obvious warning sign...)

Ice and Crusts

Finally, snow can melt and freeze. Sun or rain can affect the surface layers of snow, creating a melt-freeze layer or ice crust. On southerly aspects, multiple sun crusts forming after different snow events can cause a birthday-cake-like layering. Melt-freeze crusts tend to be persistent layers as well, and, while the crusts can be quite strong when on the surface, they can also make good sliding layers once buried. Some years they cause very few avalanches, while in other years the majority of avalanches are slides on crusts.

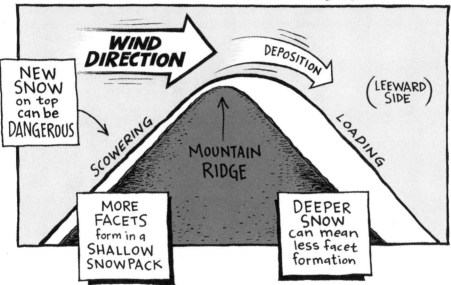

WIND DIRECTION CAN INFLUENCE FACETING

WIND DIRECTION

DEPOSITION

NEW SNOW on top can be DANGEROUS

SCOWERING

(LEEWARD SIDE)

LOADING

MOUNTAIN RIDGE

MORE FACETS form in a SHALLOW SNOW PACK

DEEPER SNOW can mean less facet formation

BEFORE YOU LEAVE THE HOUSE

Gathering Information

The first thing to do before heading out for a ski is check the avalanche forecast and weather report. There are forecast centers around the country that provide daily reports for back-country travelers. If you are new to an area or are unfamiliar with your local resources, you can go to avalanche.org to find out the contact information for the nearest forecast center.

Avalanche.org also has a list of avalanche accidents, which can be a sobering, but useful, source of information if you are visiting somewhere new. The details of these accidents help fill in the blanks in your history of the local snowpack.

The forecast center will give you a rating (see North American Danger Scale on page 32), a weather report, and an assessment of what they feel the problem for the day will be. You can use this information to help you determine where to go for a ski tour. This is the preplan part of your day. It's when you and your partners look at the first pieces of the puzzle—the past, current, and forecasted weather; the avalanche hazard for the day; and the history of the snowpack—and make a decision about what kind of terrain is appropriate for the conditions. So, for example, if it's been nuking snow, the winds are blowing at high elevations, and the avalanche hazard is considerable or higher, you should probably opt for some low-elevation tree skiing. You don't have to stay home, but you are advised to stay in simple terrain where you have a lot of route and slope options and can avoid exposure to avalanche paths.

If, on the other hand, it's sunny, calm, and dry with a low-hazard avalanche rating, you might opt to head into complex terrain. I go to these places with the understanding that I have few—or sometimes no—options to avoid exposing myself to slide paths and terrain traps, so it's only appropriate for me to be there when I have total confidence in my ability to assess conditions and keep myself out of trouble.

The information you gather in the comfort of your house is just a starting point. It helps you plan your ski day to be in the proper terrain for the conditions. Sometimes it will be clear that you only want to venture into low-angle terrain, while at other times you know the snowpack is bombproof and you can push your personal risk envelope as far as you like. Always keep in mind, however, that low hazard does not equal no hazard.

Usually conditions are somewhere in between red and green. Depending on which end of the spectrum it is (yellow-green or orange), you may want to hedge your bets and head for terrain that gives you a lot of good options to appropriately up the ante or tone it down in response to what you find in the field.

If you are in a new area and there is no information available, then it is smart to plan your first tour of the area in simple terrain. Your goal for this tour should be to gather as much firsthand information about the snowpack and the area as possible to help inform you as you plan future tours. In fact, it is probably a good idea anytime you are in a new area to do this; that way you can make more sense of the background information (your preplan) that you gathered beforehand.

Keeping Notes

I don't write notes about my ski days or the snowpack unless I'm working in a professional capacity, but many people do. The value of this habit is that you have a quick reference to help you figure out trends and pick out where the skiing should be good. You can do this in your head too, which is what I tend to do. I'll make a mental note of the conditions I encounter when I'm out and use that information to guide me on my next tour. So crusts on south-facing slopes one day may drive me to more northerly aspects the next, and winds aloft will often send me into the trees down low. I tend to ski almost every day in the winter, so I'm constantly accumulating knowledge. If your schedule is more sporadic, you may want to keep more formal notes.

North American Danger Scale

Danger Level	Travel Advice	Likelihood of Avalanche	Avalanche Size and Distribution
Extreme	Avoid all avalanche terrain.	Natural and human-triggered avalanches certain.	Large to very large avalanches in many areas.
High	Very dangerous avalanche conditions; travel in avalanche terrain is not recommended.	Natural avalanches likely; human-triggered avalanches very likely.	Large avalanches in many areas or very large avalanches in specific areas.
Considerable	Dangerous avalanche conditions; careful snowpack evaluation, cautious route-finding, and conservative decision-making essential.	Natural avalanches possible; human-triggered avalanches likely.	Small avalanches in many areas, large avalanches in specific areas, or very large avalanches in isolated areas.
Moderate	Heightened avalanche conditions on specific terrain features; evaluate snow and terrain carefully and identify features of concern.	Natural avalanches unlikely; human-triggered avalanches possible.	Small avalanches in isolated areas or extreme terrain.
Low	Generally safe avalanche conditions; watch for unstable snow on isolated terrain features.	Natural and human-triggered avalanches unlikely.	Small avalanches in isolated areas or extreme terrain.

Choosing Your Partners

It is just as important to carefully choose your ski partners as it is to knowledgeably choose your terrain. A good partnership with folks who are skilled in avalanche assessment and have similar risk tolerance can make for great tours, whereas the opposite at best is no fun and at worst can lead to serious consequences. It is nice to be able to trust the people you are with and have confidence in their abilities, experience, and communication skills.

Sometimes, however, those qualities can be difficult to discern. All too often parties of skiers form over beers, with little consideration given to the seriousness of their planned endeavor. I don't mean to overstate this. There are plenty of places you can ski with a bunch of buddies that have low or no consequences, but it's easy to underestimate the seriousness of skiing in avalanche terrain and take things for granted with your partners. So if you are skiing with someone new, stop and talk before you head out.

The conversation you have can help you determine if you even want to ski with an individual, and, if so, what kind of terrain is appropriate for your team. These days there are lots of really talented skiers who can tackle radical terrain with ease, but that doesn't mean they have any avalanche awareness. Don't let yourself get sucked into a bad decision by succumbing to desire over common sense.

Things to Ask in a Pre-Trip Conversation

- What is each person's avalanche training?
- Is everyone practiced with using a transceiver?
- Has anyone ever been caught in an avalanche? What did they learn?
- How will we make decisions as a group?
- What is our goal for the day?
- How will we change that goal if circumstances change?
- What's our contingency plan if things go wrong?

Team Numbers

How many people make up a good-size team? The more numbers you have the more potential rescuers you have in case of an accident. The downside is that decision-making gets more complex, and it is harder to manage a bigger group. If I planned to ski with more than five people, I would seriously tone down my tour to easier terrain and call it more of a social experience. Five folks are kind of my max and really only works well when we are all experienced and respectful of one another. Groups of three or four strike the best balance for me. Skiing with one other partner (especially when the two of you have lots of faith in each other gained from experience) can be a real joy, but you need to realize that rescue options are much more limited.

Going it alone is not advisable in avalanche terrain. People do it, and I must admit I ski by myself at times, but I tend to be pretty darn conservative when I go out alone. There's no one there to watch your back, no one to dig you out if you make a bad decision, and no one to help if something goes wrong. I tend to stick close to the road in these situations, with the idea being that maybe I could drag myself to the highway if I broke a leg. I still always carry my avy gear so I could help someone else out if needed, and hopefully they would do the same for me.

Gearing Up

Anyone who travels in avalanche terrain should carry basic avalanche rescue equipment, which means a transceiver, a shovel, and a probe.

Transceivers (aka Beacons)

Your chance of being found alive decreases with every minute you are buried. The fastest, most reliable way of finding someone buried in snow right now is with an avalanche transceiver. Statistics show that you have a 90 percent chance of being found alive if you are found within the first 15 minutes. That likelihood drops to 30 percent after 30 minutes.

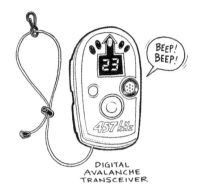

DIGITAL
AVALANCHE
TRANSCEIVER

There are currently many models of transceivers available on the market. All models made since the late 1980s operate on the same frequency–457 kHz–which means all are compatible. Most popular models are digital and provide you with an LED display indicating how far you are from another transceiver, making them relatively easy to use–even for the most novice of us.

But that said, beacon searches require practice to ensure competence. I like to start each ski season digging up some buried transceivers with my partners to brush up on our skills.

There are a few things you need to do to make sure your transceiver will work properly. One is to use good batteries. When you turn on your transceiver, a number will show up on the LED display screen indicating your battery power. Theoretically, you can allow this number to run down to 30, but I have found that batteries with power at or below the mid-50s seem to drain quickly and, depending on the transceiver, lower the unit's accuracy.

Practice
avalanche rescue
as a team

Look for CLUES

probe assembled

SHOVEL   BEACON   PROBE

Transceivers rely on two or three ceramic antennae (depending on the model) to transmit and receive signals. These antennae are somewhat fragile, so take care not to drop your transceiver onto a cement floor. The other concern is frequency drift. This can happen to older model beacons. The problem with frequency drift is that other transceivers may not be able to pick up your signal. If you have an old transceiver, it may be worth checking to see if the signal has drifted. If it has, it's time to upgrade. Check online for information on frequency drift and for model reviews.

So what's the best beacon? It's the one you practice with. Being familiar with your beacon saves time, energy, frustration, and lives. There are lots of beacons on the market. I like ones that are simple to use and reliable over time. A beacon with too many features is just confusing unless you practice with it a lot.

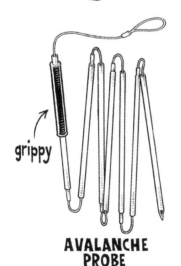

EXTENDABLE
AVALANCHE
SHOVEL

grippy

AVALANCHE
PROBE

Shovels

Lots of models of shovels are also out there. You need one that is designed for use in avalanche rescue. Your decision in determining which make and model you want should be about the type of material used in the blade and the shape and length of the handle. I am a big fan of metal shovel blades with long extendable handles because I believe they are the most effective in dense, hard avalanche debris. Sure, they may be a few ounces heavier, but in my mind that difference isn't worth the potential loss in digging ability. If I am trying to dig my best friend out of an avalanche, I want a shovel that works well.

Probes

Similarly, a probe designed for avalanche rescue work is preferable over convertible ski poles. Look for one that is easy to put together quickly. I'm not a big fan of relying on ski pole probes only, because they don't go together fast enough and often aren't long enough for big debris piles. I'm also not crazy about some of the new super-lightweight probes out there. They seem pretty flimsy and short. I would hate to have my probe break when I'm in the middle of a rescue. I am a fan of solid, reliable rescue gear.

Using only
ONE HAND
and
away from
your body

PROBING
at an
OFF-ANGLE

NOT
PAYING
ATTENTION
and
NOT
BEING
METHODICAL

PROBING LAMENESS

Other Essential Gear

Winter ski touring requires more gear to ensure your safety and comfort than what is required for a summer day hike. In addition to your transceiver, shovel, and probe, you should carry a snow saw for cutting columns in your test pits, an inclinometer for measuring slope angle, extra clothing layers, food, water, a first-aid kit, an emergency kit, a headlamp, maps, sunglasses and goggles, sunscreen, and climbing skins. See *Allen and Mike's Really Cool Backcountry Ski Book* for more information.

Text for Help

It is worth noting that texting often works better in the mountains if cell phone reception is spotty.

Cell phones can be handy in the backcountry if you need assistance, but you should know that they—and other electrical devices like MP3 players and headlamps—could interfere with avalanche transceivers. These devices seem to affect searching beacons more than transmitting ones. You might get erratic readings, hear static, or have diminished range if your transceiver is experiencing interference from an electrical device. To avoid this problem, the best thing to do is turn off your electronics whenever you put on your transceiver. You can always turn your phone back on to make a call. If you are reluctant to cut yourself off, make sure to keep your beacon a foot or so from any electronics to minimize the risk of interference.

Avalungs and Airbags

An Avalung is a lightweight tube—either worn outside your jacket or integrated into your pack—that allows you to breath when buried under snow. The tube brings air into your mouth through an intake valve near your chest and directs your exhalations away; this helps divert carbon dioxide away from the air you are breathing. Too much CO_2 and your brain tells your lungs to stop. In tests with the Avalung, buried volunteers could breathe under the snow for over an hour with no ill effects. The obvious problem with the Avalung is getting or keeping it in your mouth while being tossed and turned in an avalanche. Unless you put it into your mouth immediately after getting caught, or even before you launch yourself onto a slope, you may not be able to once you really get moving in an avalanche. There aren't a lot of statistics on this issue or on how effective the device is in saving lives, but there are enough

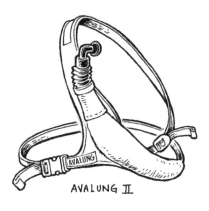

AVALUNG II

POOF

AVALANCHE
AIRBAG
SYSTEM

anecdotal stories out there to support its use. Bottom line: An Avalung is a relatively inexpensive tool that can save your life, so it's not a bad idea to use one.

Nowadays you can also get a pack with a compressed air cartridge that deploys an airbag that's activated by pulling a handle. The airbags increase your body's volume and help keep you on the surface of the snow during an avalanche. Airbags have commonly been used in Europe; in early studies, of 168 people with airbags caught in an avalanche, only 2 died. But as you've undoubtedly heard, with a little creativity people can use identical statistics to support opposing arguments. More recent studies report many cases where an airbag saved someone's life, but the numbers aren't quite as overwhelming as the European studies suggest. Airbags do keep you on the surface, but they don't protect you from trauma. If you are carried into trees or over cliffs, an airbag isn't going to save you. Still, while the numbers do not resolve the argument one way or the other, if you are one of those people who survived an avalanche because of an airbag, you probably think it is worthwhile to carry one.

The downside to airbags is they are heavy and expensive, but as they become more common and more manufacturers adapt the technology, it is likely the cost and the weight will go down. In the meantime you can mimic the effect of an airbag by wearing a large, lightweight backpack to increase your volume. This trick doesn't really add all that much volume, unfortunately, but in the absence of an airbag, it's better than nothing.

No Sure Thing

No device, transceiver, Avalung, or airbag can ensure your survival in an avalanche. Many avalanche victims are killed by trauma, especially in areas where there are lots of trees or cliff bands.

AS YOU TRAVEL

Once you have come up with a plan for your tour, it's time to head out. This step might include a drive to the trailhead if you are skiing from home, or a lift ride to the top of a mountain to access the backcountry. If you are skiing from a hut or winter camp, you may just need to open the door or crawl out of your tent or snow shelter. Now it's time to start gathering more information so you can update your assessment as you go.

Start looking around as you drive to the trailhead. Do you see any signs of recent avalanche activity? Any plumes of snow coming off the ridges and peaks above? What's the weather doing around you? Is the road wet from melting snow? Icy? Or covered in new powder? All this information helps you get a sense of what is happening in the immediate area.

Once you step into your skis and start skinning, it's time to get a bit more tactile in your assessment of conditions. Use all your senses: Look, listen, and feel. You already have some idea of what to expect based on the information you gathered from the avalanche report, local information, or your previous day's tour and weather observations. Now it's time to see how accurate that info is for your current location and the aspects and elevations you plan to ski.

Signs and Clues of Instability

Signs of instability:

- Recent avalanches
- Whumping in the snowpack
- Shooting cracks in the snowpack
- Hard snow that sounds or feels hollow underneath

Clues to instability:

- Recent heavy snowfall
- Recent strong winds
- Rapid warming
- Presence of a weak layer

You are trying to get a sense for the stability or instability of the snowpack, and we do this by looking for clues and signs. A lack of clues and signs points to stability. Of course, some clues are not always easy to find, and signs can be overlooked if you aren't paying attention. So here are some tests you can do on your tour to help figure out what is going on.

Quick and Dirty Tests on the Go

- Step out of the skin or boot track and feel the snow. How far do you sink in? Is the snow heavy or light? Do cracks go shooting out from your skis into the snow around you? How far and how quick do they go? The farther and faster they go, the more reactive the snow is to your weight. This is a sign of instability.

- Make a kick turn, then step above the lower skin track, isolating a block of snow, and see if you can get it to slide. Once again, this can give you an idea of how reactive or sensitive the snow is to your presence.

- Jump on the rollovers of small, steep slopes to see if you get any reaction.
- Take your ski pole (handle down), or better yet a probe, and push it into the snow. Use slow, steady force so you can feel resistance—or the lack of resistance. Do you have to push hard to get through a layer only to find an area with far less resistance underneath? Or does it feel

fairly consistent as you move down through the layers? A weak layer is indicated by hollow/lack of resistance areas because the snow is not well bonded, so the pole goes through the layer easily. If the pole drops suddenly as it gets close to the ground, this can indicate a layer of depth hoar down there. Ice layers feel solid when you hit them but may not be very thick. With experience you can often identify a layer of surface hoar during those years when it is well developed.

- Dig down into the snow with your hand. What do you feel? Which layers are well bonded and which aren't? How thick are these layers? Do the hard layers sit on top of the weak layers?

- Conduct a series of hand-shear tests as you travel. To do this, clear snow out from an area with your hand to make a short trench as deep as you can without taking off your skis. Above the trench, cut a square in the snow (roughly 30 by 30 centimeters, or the size of your shovel blade) using your ski pole handle. Pull on the top side of the square with your hand to see how well the upper layers of snow are bonded to those below. How much force did it take before the square of snow breaks free? Did the square crumble in your hand or did it remain in a chunk? Is the surface under the slab smooth or rough? (More discussion on this later.) This is a great test for seeing how new snow is interacting with the old snowpack.

- Cut a cornice. Use caution, though, because cornices are dangerous, especially big ones that project a long way out over the slope below. Avoid those big daddies and instead look for smaller ones to test. Ideally, choose a cornice that you can see from below or from the side so you can detect the point where it sits on solid ground and where it is overhanging. The best way to cut a cornice is for two people standing back on solid ground to toss a line—like a long piece of parachute cord with overhand knots tied at 30 centimeter intervals and maybe a few hex nuts strung in between for added cutting power—over the cornice and saw back and forth until they cut through, dropping the "bomb" onto the slope below. Other useful "bombs" include rocks or large snow turds. The larger the bomb, the more confidence you can have if it doesn't cause failure when it hits the slope below. Never cut a cornice on a slope unless you are positive that the area below is clear of people. The idea behind a cornice bomb is to suddenly load the slope. If the slope slides, then you have identified an instability, but you don't want to bury someone (or something) in the process.

Alone, a lack of instability indicated by each test does not clearly say the snow is stable, but together they help you develop a picture of what is out there and what conditions may be affecting stability. If you do get reactions, make a note of where, and then keep track of how often you get the same result in different places. One of the biggest tricks to assessing stability/instability is gaining a sense of how widespread the problem layer (if there is a problem layer) is.

Ski Cuts

Ski patrollers and ski guides commonly use ski cuts to determine if a slope is safe. The idea is to traverse in a downward sloping line across the top of a potential fracture zone. Ideally, if you trigger an avalanche doing this, you'll be able to ski out the side and off the slab. But the risk of getting caught is real. You can lessen this chance by picking narrow slopes where it is easy and quick to get to a safe area and by never trying to ski cut a hard slab, which can break much farther back than anticipated.

Here again it is important to realize that the risk of triggering an avalanche above another unsuspecting party is very real in

---

SKI CUTTING

today's crowded backcountry. The bottom line is that a ski cut is a great tool in specific situations, but you need to be certain there is no one and nothing below that could be hurt, killed, or damaged by a slide. That includes buildings, roads, vehicles, and other structures. If you cannot see the runout, the slope is too big. Ski cuts are best suited for small slopes. You can apply the knowledge gained from your cut to larger slopes with similar aspects. These guidelines are also applicable to cutting cornices.

> *Note:* Other important things to keep in mind if doing a ski cut are to make sure you have releasable ski bindings—or have rigged a way to get out of your snowboard bindings—and to remove your poles straps before beginning the ski cut. Station spotters above you to watch as you test the slope. It takes lots of experience to get proficient with ski cuts, so start small.

Finally, remember that the failure to trigger a slide does not mean the slope is safe to descend. You may just have missed the sweet spot. The information gleaned from a ski cut is simply one more piece of the puzzle. Ultimately your decision will depend on the accumulation of lots of data about the conditions.

Route-finding

Good habits and good terrain choices will keep you safe. Too many people have been killed or injured because they chose the wrong terrain for the conditions.

It's easy to get focused on whether or not the downhill slope you want to ski is safe, but don't forget, you can get in trouble on the uptrack just as easily as on the descent. Consider these points: You spend a lot more time climbing up than skiing down; typically you are wearing fewer layers so are more vulnerable to the cold; you usually have your skis locked in for going uphill so they won't release; and you have on skins, so you can't move very fast to get out of the way. All this means that the consequences of being caught in moving snow could be worse going up than going down. So choose a conservative route that avoids exposure to potential avalanches on your way to the top. Even if you feel totally confident about the snow's stability, it's important to establish good habits when you put in a route. I know of too many cases where people have been killed on the

Don't blindly follow the uptrack of others. They might have put in a lame route!

uptrack because they ventured into avalanche terrain when they easily could have climbed on safer terrain.

Good routes avoid exposure from slopes above; stay out of steep-sided gullies and terrain traps and stick to low-angle slopes and ridges. But you can't always avoid potentially dangerous slopes. If you find yourself forced to cross an obvious avalanche path or a slope that is steep enough to slide, first stop and ask yourself if you have any other options. If the answer is no, ask yourself if it is worth continuing before you jump into a dangerous situation. If the avalanche hazard is high, this might be when you turn around and go somewhere else. If you are reasonably confident in the conditions and decide to continue, you should still exercise caution and cross the danger zone one at a time, watching each other from islands of safety.

Good Route-Finding Habits

- Keep an eye on your partners and always know where they are.
- Follow ridges or low-angle, treed slopes whenever possible. Remember to consider what is above you when picking your route.

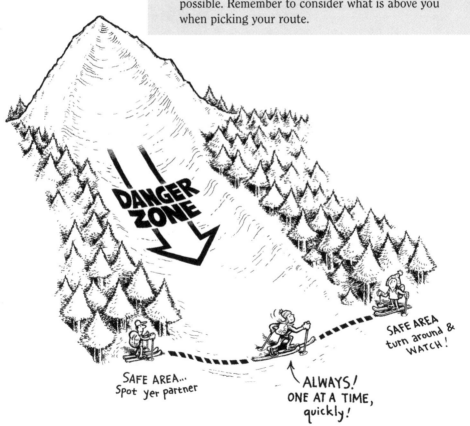

DANGER ZONE

SAFE AREA...
Spot yer partner

ALWAYS!
ONE AT A TIME,
quickly!

SAFE AREA
turn around &
WATCH!

- Stay out of steep-sided gullies or creek bottoms that can become terrain traps.
- Avoid traveling on or below cornices.
- Cross potential avalanche starting zones as high as possible.
- Move one at a time from island-of-safety to island-of-safety whenever you are exposed to potential avalanche hazard. Spot each other through exposed spots.
- Move quickly through exposed spots.
- Don't get boxed in. Allow yourself the ability to turn around if conditions deteriorate.
- Remove ski pole straps, and wear releasable bindings or have a quick way to get out of your skis or snowboard.
- Have an escape route in mind should the slope you are on avalanche.
- Don't ski above others.
- Approach potentially dangerous slopes from above so you can assess the hazard without being exposed.

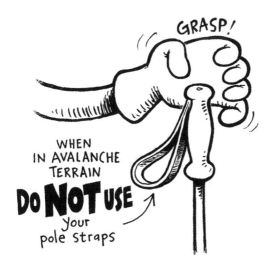

When traveling in complex terrain, it is impossible to avoid avalanche paths. Still, you can lessen your risk by going when the threat of avalanches is low, spreading out as you travel or ski (the assumption being that large avalanches are unlikely but small pockets could exist), sticking to the safest terrain possible, and using as many of the safe travel habits as are feasible.

FORMAL TESTS

You have been accumulating data on the snow's stability as you travel. As you get closer to the slope you want to ski, take a moment to pull together your observations and make a determination about conditions. Consider reviewing the avalanche triangle and assigning a red, green, or yellow light to the current terrain, weather, and snowpack. Make sure everyone in your party has a chance to share his or her observations and that they are not just going along to get along. Someone at the back of the line may have felt some whumping or seen a slide that others did not. You may decide at this point that you have enough information to make a decision. Or you may decide to do more testing.

Snowpits

Snowpits come in handy if you find yourself questioning the clues you've been given on your ascent or if you haven't been out much during the season yet and want to get a sense of what is going on below your feet. But one snowpit can be deceptive. Your best bet is to dig a couple of different pits to get a sense of how persistent and consistent your findings are. One way to do this is to have each member of your party dig his or her own pit and then share findings.

Where to Dig

A snowpit doesn't necessarily need to be dug at the top of the slope you hope to ski. I dig many pits for column tests on the approach to the ski run, but the closer I dig to the run, the more representative it will be of that specific location. Digging a pit next to the road can tell you something about the snowpack, but its relevance to stability or instability 2,000 feet up is going to be questionable.

Determining where to dig a snowpit is challenging. You want a representative slope, but you don't want to put yourself at risk. You also need to avoid areas where conditions are affected by things like trees, rocks, or wind. Ideally, look for a site mid-slope, away from trees and rocks and on the same aspect as the slope you hope to ski. Often you can find a small test slope that meets these criteria. If you can't, you can start with a quick pit in a safe area and then move out onto a more hazardous slope if your findings give you a green light. Another option is to put the person in the snowpit on belay.

Probe the area you have selected for your pit to make sure the snow depth is consistent and there are no underlying objects that will skew your results. If you find a wide variation in snow depth, it's probably worth checking both the shallow and deep areas, but focus most on the shallow spots, as they tend to be the areas from which a skier or boarder would trigger a slide.

Skiers and snowboarders are usually unable to affect snow deeper than 1 meter down, so in general you only have to dig down a little deeper than a meter to get a good sense of

the layers you need to be aware of. Of course, if your skis are sinking in 30 centimeters, you need to dig down at least 130 centimeters from the snow surface.

If it's my first pit of the season, I may choose to go to the ground just to get a better overall picture of conditions. I may also decide to dig deeper if I know there is a nasty layer down there somewhere and I want to see how it is behaving—say a February surface hoar layer or the depth hoar from a December drought.

There are three types of pits: data pits, test pits, and combination data/test pits. Data pits are what snow scientists dig. They are time consuming, as a true data pit involves collecting snow temperatures and creating a detailed snow profile. I don't do a lot of data pits unless I'm working. A test pit is simply performing one or more of the column tests that we will talk about shortly. A combo pit includes some observations of the snow layers followed by a column test.

Snowpit 101

A test or combo pit should be about as wide as a ski length. Clear away the snow (watching how your shovelfuls affect the slope below when you toss them down), and then smooth out the wall of the pit.

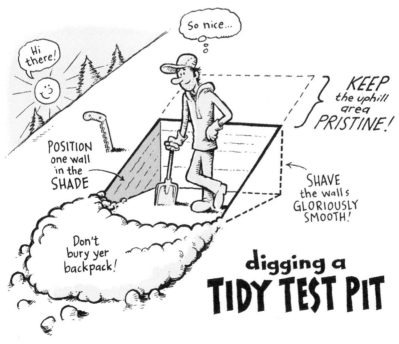

If you want to look at the layers, then do some of the following:

1. Take your gloved hand or a hat or mitten and gently brush the shaded sidewall of your pit. You'll notice that loose, soft layers of snow will fall away, while harder layers and crusts will stand out, giving you a quick impression of the snow's history.

BRUSH THE WALL
with a gloved hand
at about a 45° angle

45°

using the back of
your glove is a gentle
way to brush

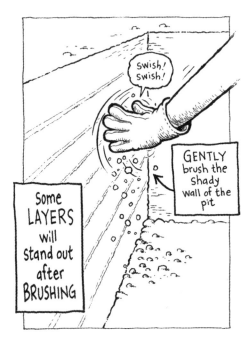

Swish!
Swish!

GENTLY brush the shady wall of the pit

Some **LAYERS** will **stand out** after **BRUSHING**

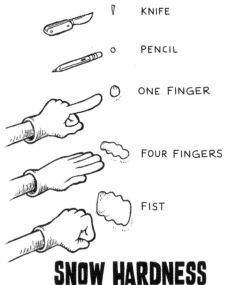

KNIFE

PENCIL

ONE FINGER

FOUR FINGERS

FIST

SNOW HARDNESS

2. Run the tip of your little finger down through an unbrushed section of the sidewall to get a sense of the resistance of the different layers. Mark these layer boundaries with your finger.

3. Check the hardness of each layer by pushing on the snow gently with, in order, your fist, four fingers, one finger, a pencil, or a knife. The difference between hardnesses is considered a step. So if your top layer is fist hardness and the next layer is four fingers, there is a one-step difference in the hardness of the two. Pushing with about two to three pounds of pressure

(just enough that you feel it in your wrist bone), you should just be able to penetrate the snow for any given hardness. If you are pushing with four fingers and feel no resistance, you would need to go to fist; too much resistance (no penetration), you would need to go to one finger or pencil and so on. This won't mean much to you until you gain experience with it, but the main idea is to get a feel for the snow and to look for problem spots,

---

like a hard slab over a soft, unconsolidated layer—an upside-down configuration that could cause problems. An ideal snowpack would gradually get harder and more consolidated as you move down, but while you might find this in a maritime snowpack, it will rarely be the case in a continental or intermountain area.

After you've felt around and looked at the snow, it's time to conduct a couple of tests to get a sense of how reactive the layers are.

Test Pits

The following tests attempt to mimic the force of a skier or snowboarder on the slope to see how the snow reacts. By carefully watching any fractures, we can learn two things about the snowpack:

1. How much force it takes to make the snowpack fail (i.e., how strong is the weak layer?). The stronger the weak layer, the less likely it is to fail. Unfortunately, strength seems to vary widely over a slope, so while it might be hard to initiate fracture at the top of the slope, you could hit a weak spot farther down.

2. What is the **shear quality** of the failure? It has been shown that the quality or energy of the shear is a better indicator of the potential for human-triggered avalanches than how much force it takes to make a weak layer fail. Think of a rubber band: If you cut it when it is fully stretched, it literally zings (or pops) apart. If you barely stretch it before cutting, it gives kind of a weak jump, and if you cut it while it is limp, nothing really happens. That's what shear quality is like. So when you conduct your tests, watch to see if a layer pops out or if it is more of a mushy failure. Does the slab slide on a smooth plane or is the break between layers rough and uneven? If you have an energetic layer that seems to want to jump into your hands, watch out. That means you have the potential for the weak layer to fail and fracture across a slope.

We use the following descriptions to quantify shear quality.

Shear Quality

Shear Characteristics	Shear Rating	What It Means
Breaks clean and fast with a smooth shear. "Pops" when it fails.	Q1	Lots of energy. Failure will easily propagate.
Breaks on a smooth plane but fails progressively or with a mushy character. Slab does not slide readily and does not appear spring-loaded.	Q2	Some energy. Failure can propagate.
Breaks on a rough or broken plane, crumbles.	Q3	Little energy. Failure unlikely to propagate.

Compression Test (CT)

The compression test is useful for measuring the strength of weak layers and, if used with shear quality, can give you information about the energy of the snowpack.

Start by isolating a column of snow 30 by 30 centimeters—about the size of your shovel blade. Make sure the column is neat and uniform. It's easy to skew your results by creating top-heavy, wobbly towers of snow. Once the column is ready, place your shovel blade face down on the top surface. Make sure the blade is flat. Now tap the blade with your hand. Start by tapping ten times with just your hand, bending at the wrist. Let gravity do the work. Watch carefully to see if you get any failure and how that failure reacts. After ten taps with no reaction, tap ten times bending from your elbow. Again, look for both failure and shear quality. If you still have no results, tap another ten times articulating from your shoulder. With all these taps you want to allow your hand or arm to drop with gravity. If you are hitting the shovel with all your might, you are hitting too hard.

Typically, people will assign a number to their results based on the number of taps it takes to make the column fail. An **easy** result (CT 1–10) indicates a weak layer in the snowpack that fails easily. A **moderate** score (CT 11–20) is that nebulous middle ground, while a **hard** score (CT 21–30) indicates a fairly strong snowpack. This information is most useful when combined with observations about the quality of the shear (was it Q1, Q2, or Q3?), as that quality indicates the energy of the snowpack in combination with its strength.

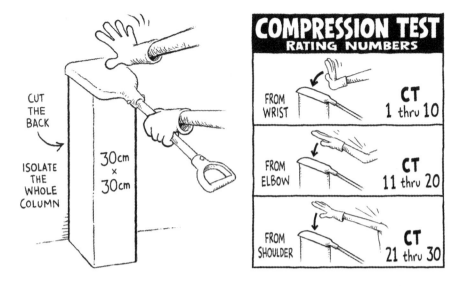

CUT
THE
BACK

ISOLATE
THE
WHOLE
COLUMN

30cm × 30cm

COMPRESSION TEST
RATING NUMBERS

FROM WRIST		**CT** 1 thru 10
FROM ELBOW		**CT** 11 thru 20
FROM SHOULDER		**CT** 21 thru 30

Compression tests give false stable scores about 10 percent of the time. In other words they indicate stability and high strength about 10 percent of the time when other factors, such as recent avalanches, indicate the snow is unstable. So it is important to do a number of compression tests to average this out. I don't do as many compression tests as I used to, since the extended column test gives me better information and is just about as quick to complete.

Compression Test Results

Results	Score
Breaks when tapping from wrist (CT 1–10)	Easy
Breaks when tapping from elbow (CT 11–20)	Moderate
Breaks when tapping from shoulder (CT 21–30)	Hard

Extended Column Test (ECT)

The ECT is a relatively new test I like, because it both indicates the snowpack's ability to fail and gives a clearer picture of that failure's ability to propagate or travel beyond the point of failure. Obviously that information is critical, as it tells you if the whole slope can fail if you get it to collapse in one spot.

To conduct the ECT, isolate a column on the uphill side of your pit that is 90 centimeters long, 30 centimeters wide, and as deep as the layers you want to test. (However, you may not

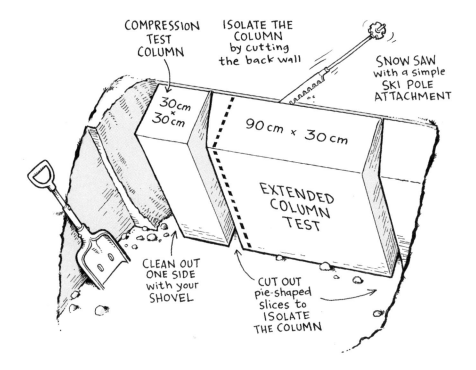

COMPRESSION TEST COLUMN

ISOLATE THE COLUMN by cutting the back wall

SNOW SAW with a simple SKI POLE ATTACHMENT

30 cm x 30 cm

90 cm x 30 cm

EXTENDED COLUMN TEST

CLEAN OUT ONE SIDE with your SHOVEL

CUT OUT pie-shaped slices to ISOLATE THE COLUMN

get the best results beyond 1.5 meters down.) To isolate the column, cut it out with a snow saw attached to a ski pole or by wrapping parachute cord around a probe placed in the back corner and sawing back and forth.

Once you have your column, take the shovel blade and place it flat on the surface of the snow just like in the CT. Begin tapping as described above: ten taps from the wrist, ten from the elbow, and ten from the shoulder. Don't use undue force. The idea is to let your hand fall of its own weight. This helps remove the subjectivity from the test. If you are pounding as hard as you can with your hand, you are exerting a lot more force than if you just let it fall with gravity.

Watch to see if the column fails and, if it does, if that failure propagates across the whole column. A positive result (i.e., the column fails and propagates across the entire column) indicates failure that can easily propagate in the snowpack and create avalanches. A positive ECT finding means the slope is unstable, regardless of how hard you have to tap (the number of taps gives you a sense of the weak layer's strength, but remember strength can vary widely across a slope; propagation sensitivity is less variable). It's a yes or no test with little gray in its results. The failure of the initial collapse to propagate all the way across the column indicates stability. The incidence of false stables with the ECT is also far less than with the CT. All slopes that produce a positive ECT result should be avoided.

Formal Tests

Extended Column Test Scores

ECTV (Extended Column Test Very Easy)	A fracture propagates across the full column during isolation.
ECTP # (Extended Column Test Propagates at Number)	A fracture propagates across the full column on the same (#) tap or one additional (#+1) tap as initiation. # is the tap that initiated fracture.
ECTN (Extended Column Test No Propagation)	A fracture initiates but does not propagate across the full column on the #th or (#+1)th tap.
ECTX (Extended Column Test No Result)	No fractures are initiated during the thirty standard loading steps.

A great thing about the Internet age is that you can go online and find videos of all these tests and more.

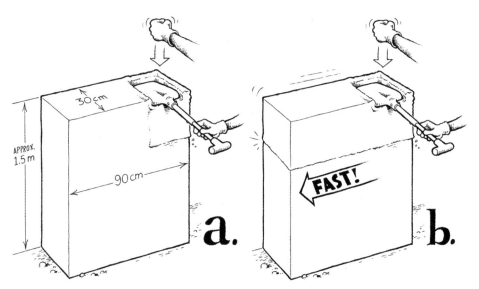

a. Weak layer fails under the shovel but no propagation across the block.
b. The initial failure propagates across the entire block, you can watch this happening, and it can happen FAST!

AT THE TOP: PUTTING IT ALL TOGETHER

Now you have lots of information, starting from the forecast you read before leaving home and ending with the tests you conducted en route. Sometimes that information is easy to interpret: Avalanches on similar aspects or whumping on the uptrack are clear indicators of danger hidden in the snow. Likewise, a long stretch of moderately warm, sunny weather with no new precipitation or wind and no signs of instability on your tour usually indicate green-light conditions. But, unfortunately, all too often things aren't that simple. It helps to have a framework to use for making decisions when conditions are yellowish, as they so often are.

ALPTRUTh

Developed by Ian McCammon, ALPTRUTh is a mnemonic acronym for simple decision-making. Ian crunched a lot of numbers and found that 92 percent of all avalanche accidents occurred when three or more of the ALPTRUTh factors were present. That means, if you find a lot of these factors on your tour, it's a sign avalanches can occur.

Here's what ALPTRUTh stands for:

A: Avalanches in the last forty-eight hours

L: Loading in the last forty-eight hours (by wind or snowfall)

P: Path (recognizable by a novice)

T: Terrain trap

R: Rating by avalanche forecaster of considerable, high, or extreme

U: Unstable snow (collapsing, shooting cracks, whumping noises, hollow sounds, poor test results)

Th: Thaw instability (rapidly warming temperatures)

If we think back to the scenario where my partner was caught in a slide, we can pull up three ALPTRUThs: We were skiing an obvious terrain trap; we'd seen shooting cracks indicating unstable snow; and the temperature had gone up markedly during the course of the day.

Chances are we've all skied slopes when three or more ALP-TRUTHs were present and nothing happened. The mnemonic is not a clear indicator of an imminent avalanche, but it's a good checklist for alerting you to the possibility of a slide, and it's quick and easy to remember and implement. You and your partner can go through the list in a matter of seconds at the top of a run.

I liken using ALPTRUTh to speeding while driving. You may speed all the time and get away with it, but on a holiday weekend when more policemen are out on patrol, your chance of getting caught speeding is higher. Noticing a lot of ALPTRUTHs on your tour is like seeing a lot of cops. You may decide it behooves you to slow down to avoid a ticket, and similarly you may decide not to ski a slope to avoid getting caught in a slide.

If you have a low tolerance for risk and have been avoiding the backcountry because you are not sure how to make decisions about when and what to ski, or if you are new to backcountry skiing and need something to help guide you as you gain experience, then ALPTRUTh is a great tool. Use it to avoid skiing slopes whenever three or more factors are present. It doesn't necessarily mean you can't ski at all; it might just mean finding a slope that does not have a terrain trap or looks like an obvious avalanche path. Or it might mean skiing certain slopes only when the avalanche danger is low and there has been no recent loading, no signs of instability, etc. Any time the combination of ALPTRUTh factors is less than three, the risk to you is low.

Stability Wheel

Another useful decision-making tool is to use a strength, energy, and structure model (called the stability wheel). Ian McCammon and Don Sharaf came up with this model to help explain the forces at work in human-triggered avalanches.

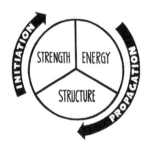

We have talked about strength and energy with our formal tests. So you already know that any time you have low CT scores (CT 1-10) and high shear-quality (Q1) or when your ECT propagates across the column (ECTP#), you have a problem. These test results indicate the snowpack has low strength and high energy. Keep in mind that whumping, avalanches, and cracking also mean strength is low and energy high.

The next thing to consider when using this model is the snowpack structure. McCammon and Jürg Schweizer identified five "lemons," or characteristics of weak layers, that are problematic in the snowpack. They found that a large percentage of human-triggered avalanches have three or more of these lemons present. So three or more lemons combined with low strength and high energy in the snowpack is a warning to stay out of avalanche terrain until something changes.

Five Structural Lemons

- Weak layer depth ≤ 1 m
- Weak layer thickness ≤ 10 cm
- Hardness difference between layers ≥ 1 step
- Weak layer grain type—persistent (surface hoar, depth hoar, facets)
- Grain size difference between adjacent layers ≥ 1 mm

The presence of a layer with lots of lemons should raise your level of concern. Often this will be the layer that reacts in your column tests, or it may be one you've been watching warily all season. While it takes experience to get good at identifying all the lemon characteristics, some will stand out in a snowpack and should be hard to miss if you are putting any effort into it.

The trickier assessments come when you don't have any of the usual signs of instability—such as cracking, whumping, or other avalanches—but you know you have a layer with three or more lemons in the snowpack. For example, let's say you know there is a layer of well-developed surface hoar that has been buried deeply. In the absence of obvious surface clues, you really need to dig a pit to get a sense of how reactive the layer is. How easy will it be to cause a fracture in the problem layer, and will it propagate beyond the initial failure?

In an example like this, you may find that the strength of the weak layer is good where you dig your pit, but because strength is highly variable, there may still be areas—or sweet spots—where it is vulnerable. This is where the energy or propagation potential of the weak layer comes in. If there is little energy, then it should be safe to ski, but if the shear-quality scores are high and/or ECT results show that propagation will occur across the entire column, then watch out.

These are the times when a test pit can really help in your assessment of the weak layer.

Layer Distribution

The distribution of these problem layers is something you should be concerned about. Some winters you may only find them at certain elevations or aspects, while other winters they may be widespread. Knowing where they are can help you evaluate the avalanche problem.

A Few Decision-Making Examples

You are out for a ski and hear lots of collapsing. You notice that on your last couple of kick turns, you got a nice large block of snow to crack loose; it didn't slide but it did drop noticeably.

Upon reaching the top of your ski run, an open slope that averages around 34 degrees, you are faced with a few choices:

- You decide to ski the run without much discussion because it is such a beautiful line. You'll probably get away with it (most of the time we do), but this only reinforces an unconscious pattern that will eventually bring you to grief unless you are really lucky.

- You decide not to dig a pit because you know you're not going to ski this run, preferring instead to find safer terrain. You've made a good decision.

- You decide to dig a pit because you want to see the layer that is reacting and what your pit test tells you, to help calibrate in your mind what instability can look like. You are learning.

- You want to dig a pit because you are hoping it will show that the slope is stable enough to ski. You are making the same mistake lots of others have made before you. There are more than enough clues pointing to instability. Trying to find something to justify your skiing the slope is just plain human.

The Human Equation

Ultimately, most avalanche accidents result from some human failure. In many cases it is easy to look with hindsight and say, "Why didn't they notice that?" "There were so many obvious clues, how could they have chosen that route?" "What were they thinking?" In some situations the victims may just have been ignorant about the hazard, but increasingly, avalanche victims have had the knowledge to assess the danger, so why didn't they get it right?

While we may never really know the story behind individual decisions, we do know that our brains are not always good at using rational decision-making tools such as the stability wheel or the avalanche triangle to make decisions, especially when desire and belief enter the picture. This is why we often ignore all the factors that don't support a desire or a belief and focus on the one factor that does. Look around and you will see people doing all sorts of things in everyday life that leave you banging your hands on your head. Funny thing is, there are probably people doing the same thing when they look at what you are doing.

Facts and figures to analyze!

Rational Thought Versus Intuitive Thought

Rational thought versus intuitive thought is basically our conscious versus our unconscious. Conscious thought is the thinking process we are aware of; it is the process we call reason, where we make choices based on outside data. It often involves collecting all the information that is available to us and then organizing and prioritizing it to come up with a decision.

Intuition, on the other hand, is part of our unconscious system. It's our instinctive reaction to a situation. Research has shown that much of what we do is determined by the unconscious system and its automatic operations. For the most part this is a good thing; it helps us navigate a complex world.

Conscious thought takes effort, more than we are usually aware of, while unconscious or intuitive thought is easy and quick. Because of this, our rational process is often undermined by our intuitive system without our realizing it. This is especially true when the situation facing us is complex with lots of factors and unknowns to take into consideration. Add in the beliefs, desires, and experiences that have shaped our lives and what we often assume is a rational decision will not stand up to any real scrutiny. There has been lots of research in this area, far more than this book is able to convey (see the appendix for more resources).

While an in-depth study of the reasons behind our decision-making is beyond the realm of this book, integrating into our knowledge base the fact that we don't always make the right (most rational) decisions when it comes to our safety in avalanche terrain is probably the most important idea you can take with you into the mountains.

So what good are the rational models discussed above? Well, in order to recognize the dangers, we need to study them and understand them. That's why we want to learn about avalanches in the first place. Structure, strength, and energy—the stability wheel—help us understand the problem. Red light/green light provides another framework for the same purpose.

Think about it this way: It's harder to make a good decision about something you know nothing about than it is to make a good decision about something you understand, even if you don't always decide perfectly. Increasing your knowledge and trying to analyze conditions is a good thing, but realize many other factors can come into play when we are at the top of an awesome powder run that can shortcut the rational process and lead us to make a decision we would think was crazy if someone else made it.

So How Can We Find a Way Around Our Desire?

If I knew the answer to this, I wouldn't need a ski budget. But there are some things that can help.

Checklists have been shown to make huge differences in producing desired results because they direct our decision-making and remind us of all the factors. So using ALPTRUTh at the top of a slope will tell you, yes, I can ski it (less than three factors), or no, I need to go elsewhere. There are a few other checklists such as the 3x3 reduction method (you can Google it), but I like ALPTRUTh because it is so simple. At this time it is unknown if there is an optimal checklist for skiing (or at least the research is yet to be done), but my guess is the day will come.

If you just can't get your head around a checklist, then a premortem test can help. In a premortem you look at your decision to ski the slope before you execute it and ask, "Okay, I ski the slope and it slides and I get buried and killed. What did I/we miss?" (I use "we" if discussing with a group—the best option—but I also find myself doing it by myself for various reasons.) The point, of course, is to pick up on the clues you were ignoring because they didn't fit what you wanted to do.

Add in a couple of other tricks to this, and I think it works even better. Next try picturing what your friends or the newspaper would say about you. This adds the element of what others will think about your decision. We are often more sensitive/ responsive to the voices of our critics. Of course, in the scenario when all the clues really are in your favor (i.e. in your examination there are no clues or signs to instability), you should have a good ski run.

Next think of what it will be like for your loved ones. Thinking of how an avalanche tragedy would affect my daughter or my wife (your mother or your brother, etc. . . .) is often the best way to make me consider the consequences of my actions. Most of us never believe that something bad will happen to us. But imagining the impact of your death on someone you care about can be a powerful way to break through your denial. It is something I often think about on the uptrack to open me up to what is really going on around me.

Lastly, skiing with a group of skeptics (especially when they are trusted friends) who are unafraid to voice their opinions can help us get beyond our desires. The more eyes and ears involved, the more information gathered. The more differing opinions and perspectives, the less likely something gets overlooked. It can often be challenging to reach a consensus decision in a group, but it will usually be a better one. A pitfall of groups, however, is when one person is more dominant or when someone is hesitant to speak up. Read enough avalanche incident reports and you will see this pattern emerge. So encourage a democracy of opinions.

More Thoughts

Desire may not just be about skiing that enticingly sick line. Your hands and feet may be so cold that all you want to do is get down and back to your car the fastest way possible. It may be the first day of sunshine after weeks of storms have kept you cooped up inside. You may not be paying attention, having abdicated the decision-making to someone you perceive to be more experienced. You may not want to make waves. You may have paid or are being paid a lot of money to ski a slope. Or you may have traveled halfway around the world for the opportunity to make a particular descent. Desires sway our opinions and color our judgment. You aren't ever going to rid yourself of their influence, but if you are aware of their effect, you may be less likely to ignore them.

Communication

It's important to be open and honest with your ski partners. Recently I was skiing out a valley in Alaska with four friends. The temperature was warm and it had not been freezing at night, so we knew we were looking at dangerous wet-slab potential as we moved down in elevation. I wanted to try traversing out to the west, staying high to avoid a steep, sunlit slope. I thought we could check it out, turning back if it seemed to be in bad shape. My desire to go west was fueled in part by the fact that we'd get to the road a lot faster going that way. My friend Dan wanted no part of that idea. He thought there was no way we could avoid putting ourselves in danger. We debated the subject for a while, until finally my wife said, "It seems as if Dan feels strongly about this, and he doesn't want to go that way. I say we respect his feelings and head east." That ended the discussion. We headed east. As it turned out, Dan was right. Even heading east, conditions were marginal. The point? Respect the conservative voices in your party. Have the courage to speak up, but also be willing to change your mind, hear others, and make concessions.

I like the saying, "Live to wimp again." You haven't wasted your time climbing to the top of a peak even if you decide to descend your uptrack. Enjoy the view, have a picnic, think of the calories you've burned, and start planning your next ski day. There is a lot of skiing to be had, as long as you don't end your life prematurely.

IF THINGS GO WRONG

Someday, regardless of your precautions, if you ski or snowboard in avalanche terrain, you or one of your partners may get caught. It's not inevitable, but it's also not impossible unless you choose to avoid all avalanche terrain. And that is a legitimate choice too. I know a number of people who are content limiting their exposure in just this way.

Even if we think our chances of getting caught are slim, it behooves us to know and practice what to do in the event things do go horribly wrong.

Ideally we are using good habits and practicing good travel techniques like crossing or skiing potentially dangerous slopes one at a time. That means only one person gets caught. If it's you, yell. Some avalanches can be surprisingly quiet. It's creepy. Yell so your buddies know what's happening and can watch you. If it's your partner yelling, watch him and make note of the area he was last seen. Pick out a landmark to help you remember.

If You Are Caught

If you find yourself in an avalanche, try to stay on your feet. Point your skis downhill at a 45-degree angle to the closest edge of the slab (or whichever way you are pointed if you don't have time to look or turn) and try to escape to the side. If you make it out, breathe a big sigh of relief.

If you don't make it or you get knocked over, keep fighting and working to get to the side of the slide. Try to jettison your skis and poles (why it's wise not to ski with your pole straps around your wrists in avalanche terrain). Skis with releasable bindings will probably come off on their own once you start to tumble. Here's where snowboards or snowshoes that don't have releasable bindings are problematic. Some snowboarders rig their bindings with a ripcord that allows them to release the bindings in case of an avalanche. The key is to get this stuff off quickly, as it is likely to drag you down under the snow. Remember, your goal at this point is to stay on the surface of the slide if at all possible. If you have an Avalung, put it in your mouth. Airbags? Deploy them immediately.

At first, avalanches have a laminar flow—the snow is moving downhill in parallel layers with no turbulence—so you have a fighting chance of getting on top of the debris and may even be able to work your way off the back or side of the slide. So fight hard. Remember that every bit of snow that goes below you is not going to wind up on top of you. The farther to the side or back of the avalanche you are, the less snow there is to bury you.

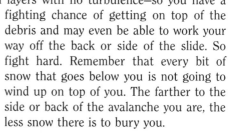

FIGHT TO STAY ON TOP!

DITCH YER SKIS if you can!

SWIM IN IT!

At some point, however, the avalanche flow becomes turbulent, and when this happens, you no longer have much chance of escaping. When you feel yourself begin to tumble, you have to decide either to keep swimming or to roll up into a ball, protecting your airway with your arm. Each strategy depends on the situation. If you feel that swimming has been useful to this point, keep it up; if there is more danger from hitting a tree or you feel utterly powerless, it might be better for you to protect yourself and your airway.

KEEP your BACKPACK ON to protect your spine

IF YOU CAN, **SWIM** TO STAY ON THE SURFACE!

DITCH your SKIS and POLES

IF YOU GET DRAGGED UNDER **ROLL INTO A BALL** To PROTECT YOUR AIRWAY!

The reality is, the snow will be moving 40 to 80 mph within four to ten seconds after it starts sliding. If you are caught in this melee, there is little you can do besides hope, pray, and fight to stay alive.

If you can't escape, then you need to prepare to be buried. As you feel the snow begin to slow down, try to protect the airspace around your mouth. Do whatever you can to keep your mouth from filling up with snow. Get your Avalung into your mouth if you have one and haven't already. If you don't have one, try throwing your arm across your face and grabbing onto the shoulder strap of your backpack to create an air pocket. If possible, punch your hand upward. It doesn't matter if you aren't really sure which way is up—just try reaching past your head. If you are successful and get your hand out through the surface of the debris, your searchers are likely to find you quicker.

If you are lucky, you'll find yourself on top when the slide comes to a stop. If you are not, your best chance for survival is to relax and trust your friends. Panicking, while totally natural, uses up precious oxygen and doesn't do anything for your survival. Most avalanche debris sets up like cement, so there is little you can do but wait to be dug out. Still, the reality is that trying to find your inner calm under these circumstances takes extreme self-control; nonetheless, it's really the only thing you can do, so try your best.

REACH UP WITH ALL YOUR MIGHT! give your rescuers something to find!

COVER YOUR MOUTH TO KEEP FROM CHOKING ON SNOW! Create an air pocket if you can.

get rid of your skis IF YOU CAN.

If Your Friend Is Caught

If you are the person watching your partner get carried away, make note of the area he or she was last seen. This is where you want to begin your search. It works best if the person who last saw the victim can stay where he or she is and direct someone else to the last-seen area. It is quite easy to lose sight of the spot. This won't always be possible, however, so it helps to pick out a landmark—an identifiable tree or rock band, something that is unique—to pinpoint the spot. If you are not sure where you saw your buddy last, be conservative and start at the top of the slide.

Before you turn your transceiver to search mode and jump out onto the avalanche slope, make sure the scene is safe. Hard as it may be to restrain yourself, it doesn't do the victim any good for you or anyone else to get caught in another avalanche. So take a moment to look around. Are there still slopes looming overhead waiting to release their load? If so, you have a very difficult decision to make. Remember your first priority is your own safety.

Once you decide the scene is safe, your next steps will be dictated by the size of your party. If it's just you, your best bet is to go to the last-seen area and begin your transceiver search. If you are part of a bigger party, you can divide up tasks. Get everyone to turn their transceivers to search mode. This is very important, as failure to switch modes can lead to confusion and wasted time if searchers are following one of the rescue party's signal rather than the victim's. Send some people to do a visual scan of the debris looking for surface clues to your victim's whereabouts. This search may locate the hand that your partner succeeded in punching up through the snow, or it may turn up skis, poles, or other items that can narrow down the search area. An avalanche victim will typically be somewhere in line with these clues.

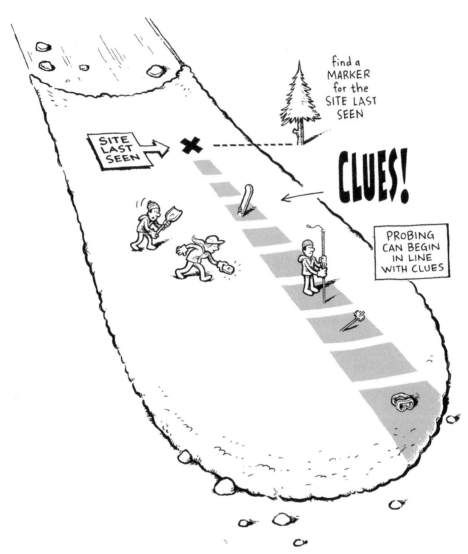

find a MARKER for the SITE LAST SEEN

SITE LAST SEEN

CLUES!

PROBING CAN BEGIN IN LINE WITH CLUES

While you are conducting your surface search, take a moment to pick up anything you find to make sure it is not attached to the victim. Check your transceiver to see if you're getting a signal and probe the area quickly just to make sure no one is buried beneath your feet. Leave the clue you found on the surface to help create boundaries for the rest of the rescue team.

Surface searchers should also do quick checks of spots where a person could get caught or snagged. Look above rocks or trees or in places where the snow slowed or eddied out. Do a quick transceiver check and probe around a bit at these spots to confirm no one is buried under there.

Transceiver Search

Meanwhile the primary searcher will zigzag down the slope below the last-seen spot trying to pick up a transceiver signal. Once you get a signal reading, move quickly in the direction of the arrow. When your digital reading shows 20 meters or less, begin to slow down. At 10 meters, slow way down and begin moving carefully and precisely, keeping your beacon aligned with the flux line and watching the transceiver numbers go down.

Once you hit 3 meters, take off your skis (if you haven't already) and begin searching in line with your last direction of travel (if you were careful enough, this should line up with the direction your skis were pointing when you took them off). Find

---

the lowest reading along the line, and then check to the sides to see if there is a lower reading. Continue to search in a grid until you home in on your lowest reading. Take your time. Move slowly and methodically. Thirty seconds to a minute spent pinpointing your search is a much better use of your time than digging furiously a meter away from your victim.

Once you have identified your lowest reading, pull out your probe and find the exact location of your victim. Probe perpendicular to the slope in an expanding spiral until you get a strike. Leave the probe in place and begin digging in from the downhill side.

If you have a buddy searching with you, have her get her probe and shovel out of her pack while you are doing your transceiver

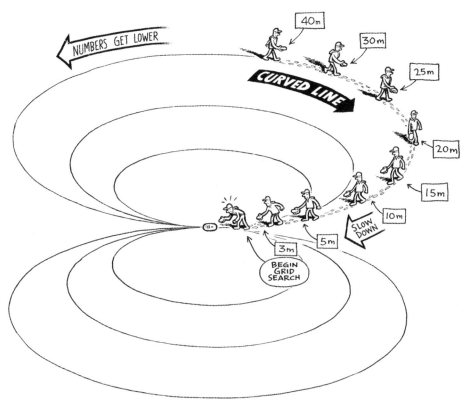

FOLLOWING the INDUCTION LINE TO A BURIED BEACON

Induction lines flow off a beacon in circular patterns so you'll almost always walk in a curved line.

If Things Go Wrong

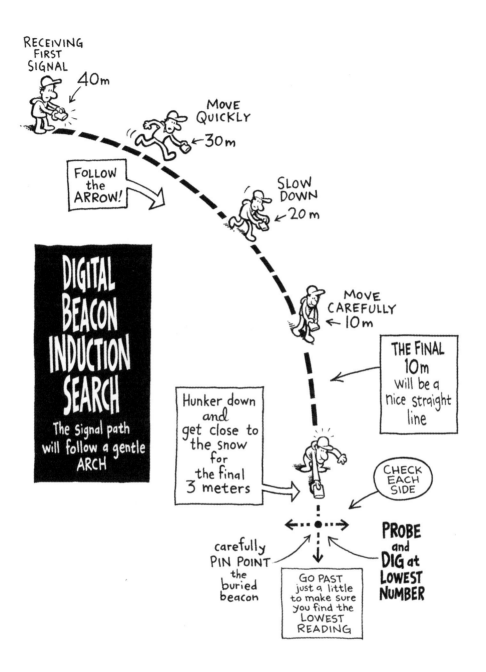

search. Once you get down to 3 meters, she can begin probing in a line out in front of you as you narrow down the search area. This may allow you to pinpoint your victim more quickly.

Digging

Most people dig the wrong way. They take their shovel and start excavating a narrow hole straight down. Not only will you be unable to extract a person through such a narrow opening, you'll also be standing right on top of them, further compressing the snow and making it harder for them to breathe.

Instead, stand downhill of your probe and dig horizontally toward it, coming into the victim from the side and clearing a wide trough as you go. If you have a number of rescuers, form a V-shape, like a flock of geese. The shoveler at the apex of the V will be doing the most work moving snow back and away from the probe, while those behind slide the snow down the middle, clearing a wide area for extracting the victim. To conserve energy, rotate positions frequently—say every 60 seconds or so.

Once you reach the victim, your priority is to find his or her head to clear the airway. Suffocation is one of the leading causes of death in avalanches. A person only has a few minutes of life without oxygen, so move quickly. After you've restored breathing (hopefully), you can continue to excavate the person. Treat the victim for the ABCDEs (Airway, Breathing, Circulation, Disability, and Environment). Stop bleeding, manage traumatic injuries, treat for shock, keep people warm, and call for help evacuating the individual from the backcountry.

LOWEST BEACON READING

PROBE OUTWARD in a SPIRAL PATTERN

Multiple Victims

Now you've really screwed up. If more than one person is buried, your chances of a successful rescue diminish. Most modern beacons have a feature that allows you to block out conflicting signals so you can home in on one person, find him or her, and then move on to the next. It takes practice to learn how to use this feature, and unfortunately, it is not always effective.

Another technique is to conduct a micro-strip search. This search pattern involves traversing horizontally back and forth across the debris pile in lines approximately 2 to 5 meters apart. These narrow bands allow you to pick up individual signals as you go, making it less likely you will have to climb back uphill to look for someone you missed.

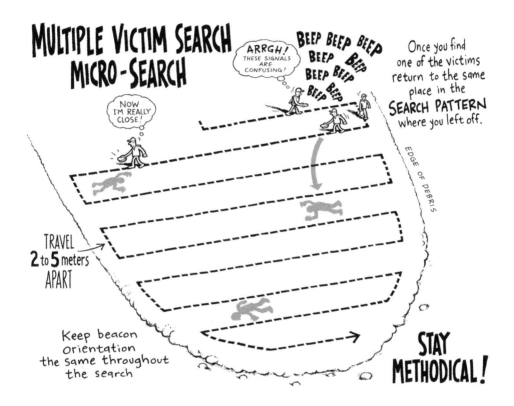

APRÈS-SKI

After you return home from a ski and have showered and eaten, it's a good time to take a moment to review your day. You don't have to be overly formal about this process, just take a moment to reflect on what went well and what did not over the course of the tour. Ideally you will do this with your ski partners, but self-reflection is valuable too.

Consider not only your decisions, but also what you observed and how those observations may affect tomorrow's skiing. Talk to your friends about what they saw. It's all part of a process of gaining information and experience to help guide you on your next journey out into the snow.

I sometimes find upon reflection that I gave into my desire to ski on a particular day more than I should have. The more I recognize this at the end of the day, the better I get at recognizing it during the day in the mountains as well, especially in my partners. Hopefully this process will alert me on that one day when my desire to ski is masking the danger lurking below.

Appendix: Resources for More Education

Books

Daffren, Tony. *Avalanche Safety for Skiers and Climbers.* Seattle: Cloudcamp, 1992.

Fredston, Jill, and Doug Fesler. *Snow Sense: A Guide To Evaluating Snow Avalanche Hazard.* 5th ed. Anchorage: Alaska Mountain Safety Center, Inc., 2011.

Haegeli, Pascal, and Ian McCammon. *The Avaluator: Avalanche Accident Prevention Card.* Revelstoke, BC: Canadian Avalanche Centre, 2006.

Kahneman, Daniel. *Thinking Fast and Slow.* New York: Farrar, Straus and Giroux, 2011.

Lehrer, Jonah. *How We Decide.* New York: First Mariner Books, 2009.

McClung, David, and Peter Schearer. *The Avalanche Handbook.* Seattle: Mountaineers Books, 1993.

O'Bannon, Allen, and Mike Clelland. *Allen & Mike's Really Cool Backcountry Ski Book: Revised and Even Better! Traveling and Camping Skills for a Winter Environment.* Guilford, CT: FalconGuides, 2007.

Tremper, Bruce. *Staying Alive in Avalanche Terrain.* Seattle: Mountaineers Books, 2008.

Wegner, Daniel M. *The Illusion of Conscious Will.* Cambridge, MA: Bradford Books, The MIT Press, 2002.

Websites and Periodicals

The *Avalanche Review* is a trade and scientific journal serving the membership of the American Avalanche Association (AAA), a nonprofit organization: americanavalancheassociation.org.

Link to avalanche forecast centers, resources, and course providers in United States: avalanche.org.

Canadian Avalanche Centre: avalanche.ca/cac.

SnowPit Technologies was founded in 1998 as a supplier of equipment and education to the snow science community and backcountry travelers: snowpit.com/index.htm.

Index

About the Author and Illustrator

Allen O'Bannon grew up in Portland, Oregon, and has been in the field of avalanche education for many years teaching level one, two, and three courses. His goal is always to keep his head above the snow, although he has been known to do head plants now and again, all in the interest of getting a closer look at the snowpack, of course.

Mike Clelland! never went to art school, he studied *MAD* magazine instead. Mike grew up in the flat plains of Michigan, then spent ten years (as a yuppie!) in New York City. In 1987 he thought it might be fun to be a ski bum in Wyoming for the winter. Unfortunately, after living and skiing in the Rockies, he found it quite impossible to return to his previous life in the Big City. Mike is presently living in a shed in Idaho where he divides his time between illustrating and being in the mountains. His passions include telemark backcountry skiing, ultralight backpacking, old movies, and cats.